Provider Sponsored Organizations

Emerging Opportunities for Growth

Allan Fine
Senior Manager
Ernst & Young LLP
Chicago, Illinois

Colleen E. Dowd
Vice President
Baptist Saint Thomas Health Associates
Nashville, Tennessee

AN ASPEN PUBLICATION®
Aspen Publishers, Inc.
Gaithersburg, Maryland
1998

Library of Congress Cataloging-in-Publication Data

Fine, Allan.
Provider sponsored organizations: emerging opportunities for growth / Allan Fine, Colleen E. Dowd.
p. cm.
Includes bibliographical references and index.
ISBN 0-8342-1177-7
1. Medicare. 2. Provider-sponsored organizations (Medical care)—United States.
I. Dowd, Colleen E. II. Title.
RA412.3.F56 1998
362.1'0425—dc21
98-28499
CIP

Orders: (800) 638-8437
Customer Service: (800) 234-1660

About Aspen Publishers • For more than 35 years, Aspen has been a leading professional publisher in a variety of disciplines. Aspen's vast information resources are available in both print and electronic formats. We are committed to providing the highest quality information available in the most appropriate format for our customers. Visit Aspen's Internet site for more information resources, directories, articles, and a searchable version of Aspen's full catalog, including the most recent publications: **http://www.aspenpublishers.com**
Aspen Publishers, Inc. • The hallmark of quality in publishing
Member of the worldwide Wolters Kluwer group.

Editorial Services: Joan Sesma
Library of Congress Catalog Card Number: 98-28499
ISBN: 0-8342-1177-7

Printed in the United States of America

1 2 3 4 5

Table of Contents

About the Editors

Allan Fine is a Senior Manager in Ernst & Young's Health Care Consulting practice in Chicago, Illinois. He serves in a leadership role in the firm's Strategy, Managed Care, Marketing, and Integrated Delivery Systems practices. He has extensive experience in strategy, developing managed care strategic plans, strategic partnering, postmerger integration, new product/service development, and developing and implementing integrated systems.

Prior to joining Ernst & Young, he served as Vice President and Director of a national consulting practice and hospital management company focused on managed care and physician–hospital integration strategy development and implementation. He has also held management positions with a provider-sponsored PPO and a major insurance carrier.

He is a frequent speaker and writer on topics related to managed care strategy, integrated delivery systems, relationships between providers, employers and managed care organizations, and marketing and sales strategies. He is the editor of the journal *Managed Care Quarterly*, senior editor of the newsletter *Executive Solutions for Healthcare Management*, and the editor of the book *Integrated Healthcare Delivery Systems: A Guide to Successful Strategies for Hospital and Physician Collaboration*. He is also coeditor of the book *Integrated Healthcare Delivery Systems: Business and Legal Forms* and co-author of the book *Dealing Direct: A*

Business Strategy for Business-Provider Partnerships. Mr. Fine is the author of chapters that have been published in *The Managed Health Care Handbook*, Third Edition; *Integrating the Practice of Medicine*; and *Hospital Strategies in Managed Care 1999*. He also serves on the editorial boards of multiple managed care and health care publications.

Colleen E. Dowd is Vice President of Baptist Saint Thomas Health Associates, an organization providing managed health care services to 11 hospitals, 430 physicians, 8 IPAs, and 20 ancillary companies. Prior to joining Baptist Saint Thomas Health Associates, Ms. Dowd held positions as Vice President of Managed Care for a large health system, Vice President of Development for a national consulting firm, and Assistant Administrator of a 220 bed hospital.

Ms. Dowd currently serves as President of the Middle Tennessee Healthcare Executives Association and was a member of the Board of Directors for the American Hospital Association's Society for Healthcare Strategy and Market Development. She serves on the editorial advisory board of *Managed Care Strategies* and as Associate Editor of *Managed Care Quarterly*. A nationally regarded speaker. Ms. Dowd has conducted presentations for numerous organizations, including the American Hospital Association, Virginia Physical Therapy Association, HFMA Dixie Institute, Georgia Society for Managed Care, Indiana University, and Tennessee Association of Homes for the Aging.

Ms. Dowd received the state of Tennessee's 1997 Young Healthcare Executive of the Year award. She holds a Bachelor of Science degree from the University of South Carolina and a Master of Health Science degree from The Johns Hopkins University.

About the Authors

William Anderson, MD, is Director of Physician Networks for Baptist Hospital in Nashville, Tennessee. He is also in private practice, specializing in the area of general and thoracic surgery.

Bruce M. Fried, formerly the Director of Health Plans and Providers at the Health Care Financing Administration, is a partner at Shaw Pittman Potts & Trowbridge in Washington, D.C. He specializes in health care matters, including advising managed care organizations on complex regulatory and other issues.

Bruce Gosser is the President and COO of Heartland Physicians Health Network, Inc., a physician-sponsored managed care company throughout the state of Kansas. Mr. Gosser was previously Vice President of Managed Care for the BJC Health System in St. Louis, Missouri.

Scott Kolesar is a Senior Manager with Ernst & Young's Health Care Consulting practice in Cleveland, Ohio. His area of expertise is health care information systems and he serves in a variety of business advisory capacities to clients across the country.

Wendy L. Krasner is a Partner in the Health Law Department in the Washington, D.C., office of McDermott, Will & Emery, an international law firm with approximately 725 attorneys. She is in charge of the firm's managed care practice. Ms. Krasner's primary activities include representation of HMOs,

PPOs, PHOs, integrated delivery networks, and multi-specialty medical group practices.

Michele Manfreda is a Legislative Research Analyst with Ernst & Young in Washington, D.C. Ms. Manfreda follows public policy issues impacting Medicare and health insurance.

Patrick K. O'Hare is a Partner in McDermott, Will & Emery's Washington, D.C., office and heads its integrated delivery system practice. He represents clients with respect to Medicare and Medicaid reimbursement appeals and litigation, corporate structuring, tax-exempt financing, acquisitions, faculty practice plans, and the overall structuring of hospital–physician relationships.

Daniel M. Scheibenreif, FSA, MAAA, is a Principal with Milliman & Robertson, Inc., in Chicago, Illinois. He has consulting expertise in the areas of health reserve and liability analysis, financial forecasting, employee benefit plan funding and compliance, and actuarial systems development.

Barry S. Scheur, JD, is Founder and President of the Scheur Management Group, Inc., a health care management and consulting firm in Newton, Massachusetts, specializing in the conceptualization and implementation of innovative and effective managed care solutions.

Michael Treash is a Senior Manager in Ernst & Young's National Health Care Practice in Washington, D.C., where he follows trends in health care policy and managed care. Prior to joining Ernst & Young, Mr. Treash worked within the HMO industry and with the Health Care Financing Administration.

Dave Vreeland is a Manager with Ernst & Young's Health Care Consulting practice in Chicago, Illinois. He oversees large projects with both technology and operational components.

Janice H. Ziegler is a Senior Associate at Shaw Pittman Potts & Trowbridge in Washington, D.C. She specializes in health care matters, including advising managed care organizations on complex regulatory and other issues.

Kimberly Zinman is a Senior Consultant with Ernst & Young's Health Care Consulting practice in Philadelphia, Pennsylvania. She has extensive experience working with managed care organizations.

Introduction

Allan Fine and Colleen E. Dowd

As providers struggle to identify mechanisms to serve the Medicare population, the Medicare program continues to evolve. In addition, the Medicare beneficiary population is anticipated to experience continual growth. It is clear that the federal government is creating opportunities for private enterprises to get more involved in the direct funding of Medicare.

Through the Balanced Budget Act of 1997 (BBA), the Health Care Financing Administration (HCFA) is introducing a range of new options for financial institutions, for-profit health care ventures, and providers to participate more actively in the funding and delivery of care within the Medicare program. In addition, Medicare beneficiaries are expected to be more educated and involved in the delivery of the health care services they receive. HCFA's 1998 Beneficiary Information Campaign will "kick off" a widespread educational initiative, and in fact there is expected to be an annual campaign as a way for the federal government to communicate important information to Medicare beneficiaries.

The dynamic nature of the Medicare program makes establishing Medicare provider strategies a difficult task. The private sector is vigorously reviewing possible ways of capitalizing on the changes being introduced in the financing and delivery of Medicare health care services. These changes are occurring in an array of Medicare recipient options, including:

- traditional Medicare, Parts A and B
- medical savings accounts (MSAs)
- health maintenance organizations (HMOs)
- provider sponsored organizations (PSOs)
- fee-for-service options

As financial institutions explore opportunities to become involved with MSAs, which combine individual savings accounts with high-deductible health insurance plans, providers, especially those in rural markets, struggle with the task of assessing the opportunities (and risks) that PSOs present for actively participating in managed care for the senior population, a population that is energetically enrolling in Medicare risk HMO plans (see Figure I–1).

Throughout this book, information related to regulatory, legal, and operational perspectives is outlined to enable providers to assess the pros and cons of developing and managing PSOs. In addition, fundamental strategic questions are asked to determine if a medical community not only has the desire to work together in offering a PSO but can assemble the funding, master the marketing, and manage the operation of one of these complicated managed care plans. (A prerequisite, of course, is the willingness of physicians to participate in a PSO.)

Many of the legislative changes probably are being caused by the growing demand by physicians to reestablish traditional patient-physician relationships, similar to those they believe existed prior to managed care. However, if providers are looking toward PSOs as a way to "escape" the fundamental principles of managed care, they will be disappointed. In fact, in forming a PSO, providers will have to assume most of the managed care functions that have been undertaken by HMOs. In essence, providers become a health plan.

Applications to HCFA from physicians and hospital-based groups seeking to form PSOs are numerous. The principal catalysts for the emergence of PSOs are favorable Medicare legislative changes and efforts by providers seeking alternative ways to access seniors in managed care networks. PSO development can,

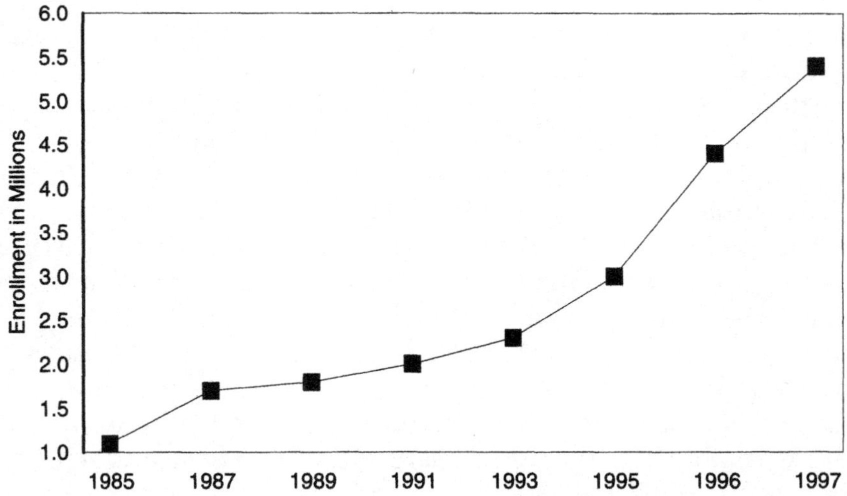

Figure I–1 Medicare risk enrollment growth. *Source:* Data from HCFA.

in part, be attributed to the perception of providers that they have been excluded from direct relationships with Medicare beneficiaries.

The most important legislative changes are those that occurred as a result of the adoption of Medicare Part C (Medicare+Choice). The revision of payment rates throughout the country, combined with the coverage choices available to seniors, affords providers a new managed care option for serving the senior population. Under Part A and Part B of the Medicare program, physicians have the prerogative of accepting Medicare payment on a fee-for-service basis. Part C is a risk product that enables providers to obtain a per member per month fee to care for seniors (and thus allows a shift from fee-for-service to risk-based reimbursement).

HCFA is responsible for overseeing many of the legislative procedures that will govern PSOs. The potential impact of PSOs on traditional managed care organizations is unknown. PSOs may form partnerships with HMOs, may become competitors of managed care networks, or both. The Congressional Budget Office estimates that one million Medicare beneficiaries will be enrolled in PSOs by the year 2002 and that nearly 10 million seniors will be enrolled in HMOs.

The same standards and contracting requirements that currently apply to HMOs apply to PSOs, with the exception of a few revisions. The revisions are intended to eliminate barriers to PSOs while enhancing quality assurance. A PSO must be organized and licensed as a risk-bearing entity that is eligible to offer health benefits coverage under state law in each state in which it seeks to operate. If a state fails to take action on a (substantially complete) licensing application by a PSO within 90 days of submission, denies licensing on the basis of discriminatory requirements, or imposes solvency standards different from those established by the Department of Health and Human Services (DHHS), the PSO can seek a federal waiver enabling it to contract directly with DHHS for Medicare enrollment on a risk basis. A waiver may be effective for a maximum of 36 months. Application for such a waiver must be made no later than November 1, 2002. After that time, all licensure will be handled at the state level.

Solvency standards established by DHHS require that a PSO's assets and the ability of its affiliated providers be considered from a delivery risk rather than financial risk perspective. Delivery risk is the degree of likelihood that members will no longer be directly provided with services if the PSO fails. PSOs will be permitted to count items such as land, buildings, equipment, letters of credit from banks, and certificates of fiscal soundness by independent actuaries as assets in determining their net worth.

The BBA establishes a minimum enrollment for Medicare+Choice of 1,500 for PSOs that primarily service urban areas and 500 for PSOs that primarily service rural areas (in contrast to 5,000 and 1,500 respectively for HMOs). DHHS can waive this requirement for a PSO, as well as the 50/50 enrollment mix requirement, which demands that a minimum of half of a health plan's enrollment consist of commercial members. Both of these requirements will be phased out after 1998.

As a result of the introduction of new Medicare beneficiary options, a whole array of new terms are being developed and used. The following chapters will define such terms as *affiliated provider, substantial portion of care rendered,* and *federal and state solvency standard.*

There still remain unanswered questions that must be addressed in order to ascertain whether PSOs are truly a viable option for most provider communities. These questions include the following:

- How can an existing provider organization (e.g., a provider-hospital organization) qualify as a PSO?
- What is a "substantially" complete PSO application?
- How much flexibility do the federal solvency standards provide?
- How will the timing of the different PSO requirements fit together?
- How will insurance companies work with (or against) PSOs?

PSOs entering into Medicare full risk contracts will be paid on a capitated basis. Rates will be established in roughly the same way as for HMOs (i.e., as a percentage of the adjusted average per capita cost [AAPCC] for the area in question).

The current capitated payment methodology used for Medicare managed care plans has been modified by the BBA, through phasing in a 50/50 blended payment of local and national costs and a minimum monthly floor of $367 per member per month. The secretary of DHHS will be permitted to enter into partial risk payment arrangements with any risk contractor. These arrangements, while providing the full Medicare benefit package, will pay contractors a combination of capitated rates and costs. The likely result is that PSOs will become more feasible in rural areas, ensuring that the Medicare program shares in savings from efficiencies.

Perhaps even more significant benefits will result from the strategic development of PSOs. In theory, providers are closer to patients; and in most cases they do not need to generate corporate profits, arguably making them better able to care for patients within the local community. On the other hand, can physicians and hospitals really work together to deliver care to an aging population with growing expectations regarding customer service and quality? Should they build the necessary health plan infrastructure or partner with vendors? Most importantly, do providers understand how risky the Medicare business is and can they operate under a financially sound PSO model?

PSOs can provide communities with provider-based managed care options to supplement the Wall Street–based options. However, it is clear that PSOs must be different (in fact better) than HMOs if providers are to get what they desire: more control over the financial and clinical aspects of delivering Medicare services.

The formation of a PSO unquestionably offers providers a great opportunity. Unfortunately, it also brings with it substantial risk. Should a PSO be successful, it can foster a very close relationship between a medical community and its seniors. However, should it fail, local providers must be prepared to live with the impact the failure may have on the entire community, including the commercially insured population and local businesses.

Strategically, providers should develop programs to serve a predetermined portion of the Medicare beneficiaries in their region. Of course, they may serve the beneficiaries through traditional Medicare, Medicare HMOs, or a Medicare Select product, but as this book shows, under the appropriate conditions, the best way may be through the formation of a PSO.

CHAPTER 1

Creating a Vision and Goals

Allan Fine

Provider sponsored organizations (PSOs) are public or private entities consisting of a provider or group of affiliated providers organized to deliver under contract a spectrum of health care services to purchasers. They are created to allow providers to contract directly with payers on a risk basis. They also afford the opportunity for providers to organize and contract directly with the Department of Health and Human Services (DHHS) for Medicare beneficiary members on a risk basis, perhaps along with other payers, obviating the need to become licensed as a health maintenance organization (HMO). It is argued that, for providers seeking risk contracts, PSOs will eliminate the middleman.

PSOs are viewed essentially as risk-contracting alternatives for government programs. The Balanced Budget Act of 1997 (see Chapters 2 and 4 for additional information on this act) authorizes their role in Medicare risk contracting. Multiple states have passed their own statutes recognizing variations of PSOs for Medicaid risk contracting.

DIFFERENCES BETWEEN PSOs AND MANAGED CARE ORGANIZATIONS

Managed care organizations (MCOs) are in the business of selling health care coverage whereas PSOs are mainly concerned with the delivery of health care services. Second, managed care organizations are paid primarily on a full-risk premium basis whereas PSOs use multiple payment mechanisms. Third, managed care organizations are typically viewed as financial intermediaries whereas PSOs are considered to be care delivery systems.

PSOs have been called "HMO look-alikes." PSOs are, at times, required to be licensed by state regulators in the states in which they operate, although typically to a lesser degree than HMOs (and they usually are not compelled to have as high a level of capitalization and reserves). In markets in which state licensure does not apply, PSOs may be considered for federal licensure for Medicare through a DHHS waiver process. It should be noted that a PSO must function like an HMO under a Medicare risk program. The PSO must possess effective administrative, medical management, claims processing, marketing, financial, member services, and other capabilities. In addition, PSOs are subject to oversight for quality of care and financial stability by state and federal regulators. It is apparent that in many markets PSOs will be in direct competition with MCOs for categories of eligible members.

The introduction of PSOs may force managed care organizations to refocus on Medicare. MCOs may decide to infuse resources from failing commercial or Medicaid products into new Medicare products. In early 1998, Aetna US Healthcare indicated that it may drop out of New York State's Medicaid programs to focus on its potential Medicare and commercial business.[1]

ACCEPTANCE OF RISK

Insurance risk generally has been the trigger for licensure and solvency requirements and regulatory oversight at the state level. The National Association of Insurance Commissioners (NAIC) in December 1996 commented on the implications of the acceptance of risk by PSOs: "All entities that assume health insurance risk must be subject to solvency and other appropriate consumer protection standards, irrespective of the name and form of the entity. Any regulatory framework should foster a level playing field among risk-bearing entities that engage in similar types of arrangements."[2]

Providers need to understand the salient risk-contracting factors, including

- *the ability to innovate:* the ability and incentive to seek more effective and appropriate care modalities for the elderly (e.g., routine physicals, geriatric assessment, health education, flu shots, and blood pressure screening not covered under Medicare)
- *the ability to identify and manage subgroups:* the initiation of a risk plan relationship with each Medicare member at the time of enrollment rather than at the time of a health care crisis (subgroups, such as high utilizers or individuals with similar diagnoses, can be identified through screening and referral)
- *the ability to focus on outcomes:* the capture of complete utilization data (because members receive all their health care within a closed system)
- *the ability to enhance provider performance:* the treatment of risk contract members by a defined pool of providers (incentives, such as extra time to visit nursing home patients to perform geriatric assessments or to make home visits, can be created)
- *the ability to contain costs:* lower premiums for Medicare beneficiaries resulting from cost controls

DETERMINING MARKET ATTRACTIVENESS FOR MEDICARE RISK CONTRACTING

Not all providers will find pursuing Medicare risk-contracting initiatives a viable strategy. Any provider tempted by risk contracting should evaluate the level of the local adjusted average per capita costs (AAPCC) capitated payment for Medicare enrollees. Markets with higher penetration tend to have high to moderate AAPCC payments. Another factor to consider is the level of commercial HMO penetration. Markets with high to moderate commercial HMO penetration tend to have higher Medicare risk penetration. In addition, the number of Medicare eligibles will impact a provider's decision to pursue Medicare risk contracting, since markets with a significant population of Medicare eligibles have higher levels of Medicare risk enrollment. Finally, the cost of care and the level of utilization of services need to be considered, as markets with lower costs of care and lower utilization levels have higher Medicare risk enrollment.

THE RISKS OF RISK CONTRACTING

Prior to entering a Medicare risk contract, providers should understand the nature of the risks inherent in the arrangement and how withholds operate (both from a financial and a practice perspective). Providers should ask the following questions in evaluating Medicare risk-contracting opportunities:

- Can we cover administrative and health care costs?
- Can we deliver care according to the health plan's admission and discharge data?
- Can we limit prescribing to drugs in the formulary?
- Will physicians adhere to clinical guidelines?

Regardless of whether providers enter into Medicare risk contracts, they cannot ignore the fact that the fastest growing segment of the health care market consists of those over age 65. Since the 1960s there has been a significant increase in the number of Medicare beneficiaries nationwide (Figure 1–1). Currently at 39 million (13 percent of the total population), the 65

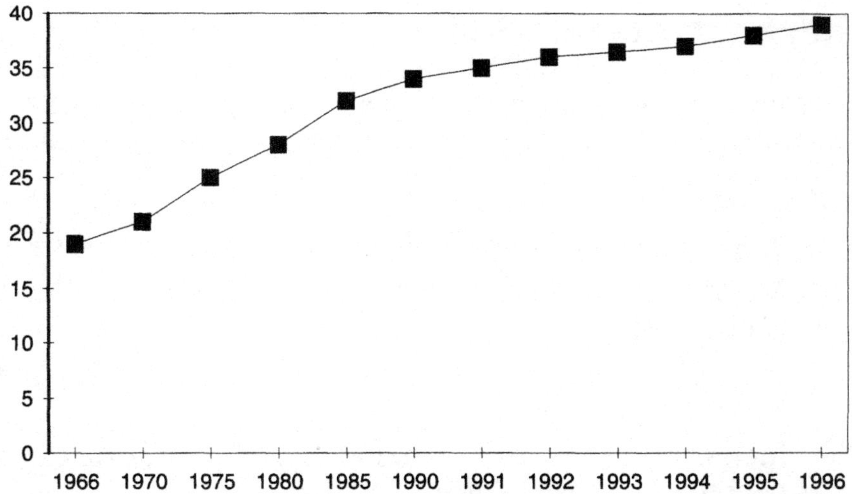

Figure 1–1 Growth in Medicare beneficiaries. *Source:* Reprinted from *HCFA Statistics Populations,* 1996 HCFA Statistics (Part I), Health Care Financing Administration, Department of Health and Human Services.

plus population is projected to grow to nearly 65 million by the year 2030. These older Americans

- account for over 25 percent of all physician services
- account for 36 percent of personal health care expenditures
- average 8.6 days per hospital stay
- occupy 50 percent of acute care hospital beds
- purchase one-third of all prescription drugs
- account for only 6 percent of HMO memberships

Increasingly, Medicare beneficiaries enrolling in risk contracts are experiencing higher satisfaction levels than in the past. Enrollees no longer have to deal with the confusing paperwork common under fee-for-service Medicare. They typically pay lower premiums than in comparable supplemental plans. In fact, they often agree to receive all of their health care through the plan and no longer use their Medicare card in other settings.

APPROPRIATE GOALS FOR PSOs

Providers contemplating the development of a PSO should establish goals and devise a plan for accomplishing them. Examples of goals include

- developing an additional Medicare-based revenue source
- keeping 100 percent of the health plan premium in the community
- channeling enrollees into provider or affiliated hospitals and medical offices
- increasing the share of premiums spent on medical care to between 85 and 90 percent
- reducing the administrative expenses of utilization management
- creating a provider-friendly health care organization
- improving payment schedules for hospitals and physicians
- regaining control of the patient-provider relationship

There are various PSO components and requisites that providers need to have in place if the PSO is to be viable, including

- a network of hospitals and physicians
- an enrolled patient population
- regional market coverage
- direct negotiation of the scope of benefits by the purchasers and providers
- capitated premiums (these place providers at risk)
- a provider-set reimbursement schedule
- a provider-managed utilization and cost infrastructure
- stop-loss, reinsurance, and out-of-area coverage to limit provider risk

- purchaser-established performance standards (e.g., "report cards")
- a purchaser-provider shared information system

SUCCESS FACTORS

Providers will need to develop or acquire capabilities in the following areas if they are to have a decent chance of developing a successful PSO:

- marketing
- member services
- financial systems (to distribute and track premium dollars)
- capital formation
- network development
- governance structures
- quality requirements, including Health Employer Data and Information Set (HEDIS) standards
- patient education
- demand management interventions
- information systems, including community health information networks

Generally, providers have been and continue to be dependent on HMOs for information systems support, eligibility management, patient education and wellness programs, and member services.

Providers intent on developing a PSO need to consider whether it is prudent for them to build or buy the infrastructure-related functions identified above. The decision to build or buy often will be influenced by cost, timing, and degree of desired control. Many providers may find that appropriate functions to be outsourced include claims processing, credentialing, medical management, and information systems management.

To successfully compete in the Medicare managed care market, a PSO must differentiate itself on more than just price. As outlined in Chapter 3, differentiating factors may include

- strong customer service and retention
- broad provider networks (which serve as PSO sponsors and as sources for caregivers)
- significant managed care managerial experience and a solid understanding of local market dynamics
- a large diversified enrollee base
- substantial financial resources
- extensive information systems

Forming a successful PSO requires providers to be able to forge an alliance with their health systems in order to cooperatively manage patient care more effectively. Frequently, capitation will form the payment framework for collaboration. Physicians and hospitals will share a risk pool to provide an incentive for reducing unnecessary utilization while protecting patients and outcomes. One way of developing a PSO is to combine the activities of a physician-hospital organization (PHO) and those of a managment service organization (MSO). Under this scenario, the PHO provides the governing structure and delivery network for direct contracting, while the MSO supplies the management capacity and managed care contracting infrastructure. The expectation is that the PSO will then have the ability to compete on the basis of both cost and quality.

STRATEGIC QUESTIONS TO CONSIDER WHEN ASSESSING THE COMPETITION

It is incumbent upon providers who are developing a PSO to be cognizant of current and potential competitors and their capacity to compete. In assessing the competition, the providers should consider the following questions:

- How will becoming a PSO affect relationships with insurers?
- How many health plans and PSOs will be in the market?
- Is the PSO's delivery system large enough to compete with Medicare HMOs?
- Can the PSO market a low premium benefit package that provides prescription drug coverage?
- Can the PSO compete with the advertising and marketing budgets of large insurers?

CAPITALIZING A PSO

Providers interested in developing a PSO may seek outside capital. Sources include venture capital firms, physician practice management companies (PPMCs), and private investors. Providers must recognize, when pursuing outside capital, that they will likely have to relinquish some control, since each source of capital will expect a specific financial return on its investment. Typical venture capitalists seek annual returns of 35 percent to 50 percent over a three- to seven-year time period, along with a viable exit strategy. A PSO will not be able to meet this criterion, principally because of the protracted break-even period as well as the small profit margins, which are not even guaranteed.

Although the start-up period is perhaps the most challenging time in which to raise capital, owing to the inherent risks in starting a new venture, the credibility of the Health Care Financing Administration (HCFA) as the payer should enhance the providers' ability to arrange for debt financing. The providers might find that a combination of inside equity and debt financing will cover the capital expenditures until the PSO achieves its break-even target. The debt interest will increase the return on equity for the PSO by providing a tax shield against earnings.

Inside capital includes money from founders and stakeholders. If there are multiple providers participating in the development and operation of the PSO, all will probably contribute funds to the PSO. The providers should note that federal and state laws regulate how funds need to be contributed. Some providers may contact banks for debt financing to assist in obtaining start-up capital; however, most banks will still require personal guarantees from the PSO's participating providers.

Conservative estimates of start-up costs for a PSO range from $3.25 million to $6 million. These costs include preoperating costs, capital expenditures, and working capital. Preoperating costs include actuarial fees, legal fees, consulting fees, salary for full-time staff, and general overhead. Capital expenditures typically include the purchase of furniture, fixtures, equipment, and a management information system capable of performing an array of managed care functions. Working capital is needed to cover initial accounts receivable, potential medical losses, general administrative expenses involving enrollment, marketing, and commissions to brokers. HMOs, by comparison, generally have substantial reserves and ready access to capital markets. The challenge for a PSO is to demonstrate that it has a sufficient level of reserves or ready access to capital, thereby assuring potential enrollees that it is a financially viable alternative to traditional HMOs.

LEGAL REQUIREMENTS FOR FORMING A PSO

Providers intent upon forming a PSO must initially form a legal organization that has authority to permit its members to participate in risk contracting (see Chapter 4 for a more extensive discussion of the pertinent legal requirements). The creation of a legal organization requires the development of bylaws, articles of incorporation, and a board committee structure. The PSO also must have a contractual agreement with each provider offering services to enrollees. Contracts are needed for primary care physicians, specialists, PHOs, ancillary providers, administrative services vendors, and pharmacies.

The agreements should specify the types of services that will be provided, the parameters within which they will be provided, and the reimbursement schedules for these services. Ideally, agreements should allow single-signature contracting for the entire network. Language in the agreements should conform with pertinent Medicare contract requirements.

DEVELOPING A FINANCIAL PLAN

It is recommended that a nascent PSO develop a financial plan for the first three years of its operation. The plan should include a medical cost model reflecting

- hospital inpatient and outpatient costs
- primary care costs
- costs for specialist services, other services, and prescription drugs
- administrative costs
- the level and funding of reserves
- a capitation plan that complies with applicable federal and state laws

The financial plan should also include a marketing analysis that encompasses a demographic description of the market, an analysis of the competition, and the anticipated enrollment for the first three years of operation.

DEVELOPING A SALES PLAN

A PSO should have appropriate sales and promotional capabilities to approach both Medicare enrollees and employers providing health insurance coverage for retirees. A significant part of the sales effort should focus on the benefit plan, which describes the types of services offered and the level of coverage that will be provided. The benefit plan also establishes policies and procedures for the provision of emergency services by network and out-of-network providers. Appropriate staff will need to be hired to handle direct marketing to individuals and employers, administer commissions to brokers and/or sales staff, and develop an advertising campaign (including collateral materials).

The next step is to develop a process for enrolling members. The PSO must create applications for enrollment and member handbooks. Other documents to be created for distribution to enrollees include certificates of coverage; a benefit plan summary describing types of services covered, copayments required, and any other member costs; and a network directory containing a comprehensive list of providers and an explanation of how to access care using the network.

ESTABLISHING CONTROLS

Upon formation of a PSO, controls are needed to coincide with guidelines and protocols associated with basic core components of the PSO, including finance, utilization management, member eligibility, claims adjudication, physician credentialing, quality assurance, and member grievance procedures.

As described in Chapter 7, the PSO needs to determine how to administer capitation payments and how providers inside and outside the network will be reimbursed. In addition, the PSO must ascertain how risk pools will be established and shared and also identify specific operational procedures for premium billing and payment.

Financial Controls

Financial control issues include

- underwriting guidelines
- hospital payment terms
- ancillary service provider payment terms
- pharmacy provider payment terms

- physician fee schedule maintenance
- stop-loss coverage or reinsurance
- tracking and reporting of financial performance for all physicians
- provider payments (accounts payable)
- premium billing (accounts receivable)
- risk funds maintenance

Utilization Management

One object of utilization management is to ensure that patient care is delivered consistently across the PSO. Members of the network must agree to adopt standardized protocols and procedures for treating patients. In addition, compliance with protocols must be monitored. Monitoring activities should focus on, among other things, primary care provider authorization for inpatient admissions, expensive tests for outpatients, and referrals to specialists.

Member Eligibility

All providers in the network should be able to identify patients who are members of the PSO and should have current information on each member, including the member's choice of primary care provider. The PSO needs to be able to track and reconcile membership and capitation data monthly. Member ID cards containing vital information must be issued. Systems also should be developed to communicate pertinent information to the PSO's participating providers.

Claims Processing

The PSO, like an HMO, needs to process claims. The relevant functions include coordinating claims payments with the utilization review approval process, adjudicating claims using policies and procedures common to HMOs, adjusting provider payments according to contractual arrangements, issuing claims payment checks, and coordinating benefits (where applicable).

Provider Credentialing

Credentialing and recredentialing procedures are the means by which the PSO can ensure that network providers comply with medical management and quality assurance protocols.

Quality Assurance

The PSO must implement policies and procedures and tracking mechanisms to ensure that it is meeting National Committee for Quality Assurance (NCQA) standards. (Note that these standards entail the need to perform a certain number of outcome studies.)

Member Grievance Procedures

The PSO will need to develop protocols and procedures for accepting and adjudicating complaints. The grievance procedures must offer multiple levels of appeal, establish standards for resolving grievances in a timely manner, and meet HCFA requirements.

The Management Information System

The management information system (MIS) is critical to the PSO's ability to manage risk (see Chapter 7 for a more comprehensive discussion of the role of an MIS in developing a PSO). At a minimum, the MIS should have

- the ability to track physician education, board certification, licensure, and employment history

- a core managed care claims system that supports enrollment and eligibility management, premium billing, capitation funds management, and claims processing and reporting
- a data analysis and provider-profiling system for tracking network and individual provider performance
- electronic data interchange capability for transmitting eligibility information, referrals and authorizations, claims submissions, and claims inquiries

STRATEGIC IMPLICATIONS

As discussed earlier, one of the most challenging issues that providers confront when creating a PSO is whether to build or buy the necessary infrastructure. Factors to consider include capital requirements, the length of the commitment, the competitive environment, the relationship of the infrastructure to other elements of the organization's strategic plan, and the relative importance of "speed to the market."

The PSO will need to develop a plan for providing out-of-area coverage (e.g., subnetworks to meet coverage requirements). In addition, it will face demands to link with other PSOs.

Familiarity with the HCFA approval process is essential for delivering services to the Medicare segment and for understanding how to manage high-risk populations effectively. The marketing of Medicare products, particularly point-of-service plans, requires benefit design alterations and appropriate packaging of the benefits.

Customer education and retention programs need to be in place. The PSO needs to place a strong emphasis on health outcomes, managing high-risk care and treating both acute and chronic conditions, and adhering to federally mandated regulations. The PSO should consider conducting market research for the purpose of gaining insight into how to develop a marketing plan for the Medicare product. Patient satisfaction, which can be measured qualitatively and quantitatively through market research, often has major financial implications. According to industry standards, the incremental loss of 2 percent of enrollment equates to a loss of approximately $1.8 million.

One of the most significant mistakes made by PSOs, and perhaps the reason that many fail, is underestimation of the requirements for becoming a managed care organization, particularly the necessary investment in information systems. Many PSOs are unable to build an adequate system because, in order to leverage the investment, they need a large market base, which is not always available.

An option that is more attractive for some providers is to contract with a Medicare risk HMO. Some providers prefer this option because this type of HMO will have experience in Medicare risk contracting, will have an infrastructure capable of supporting Medicare lives, will have a track record of empowering physicians, and will be capable of adding value (by offering access to capitated Medicare lives). Any provider contemplating this option must, however, carefully evaluate the implications of contracting with a Medicare risk HMO from, at a minimum, operational, financial, marketing, and medical management perspectives prior to pursuing such a contract.

The emergence of PSOs creates more competition in the market, increases beneficiary enrollment in managed care, expands Medicare managed care into new markets, and appeases providers, who have suffered from payment reductions on the fee-for-service side. Developing a PSO represents a strategic decision by a provider to enter the buyer side of the Medicare managed care market. As discussed in this chapter, the competitive and financial risks of starting a PSO are significant. Although the immediate goal may be to compete directly against health plans for control of Medicare covered lives, the development of a PSO might be part of a more comprehensive strategy to enter and eventually compete in all health insurance markets.

To effectively compete in the Medicare managed care market, the PSO needs to achieve price parity with the HMO competition. The PSO may in some instances benefit from its provider-owned status; however, in order to grow and sustain a large Medicare membership, it must be price competitive. Matching managed care organizations on price requires the PSO to match the cost management capabilities of these organizations. On the medical expense side, the PSO, like an HMO, needs to align incentives and impose a level of discipline in order to meet utilization and cost targets. On the administrative side, the PSO must achieve the same efficiencies as HMOs in the areas of membership, claims and appeal processing, information management, network contracting and maintenance, and regulatory and legal affairs.

A CRITICAL STRATEGIC PLANNING ISSUE

Many providers have devoted substantial resources to the creation of PHOs and the establishment of primary care networks to deal with managed care and the assumption of risk. Medical staffs and hospital management have been vocal about their desire to contract directly and eliminate the intermediaries (i.e., managed care organizations). Many integrated delivery and financing systems, however, have limited enrollment of full risk covered lives, while managed care organizations continue to transfer risk to hospitals and physicians. This is principally true for the commercially insured population and, increasingly, the Medicaid population.

Medicare has remained primarily in the fee-for-service category, except in limited markets throughout the country, and it has by default become one of the better payers. Perhaps even more significant is that it remains the dominant payer, accounting for half or more of hospital revenues and a substantial portion of most physicians' revenues.

Significant strategic issues associated with PSO development need to be addressed by hospitals, physician groups, and integrated delivery and financing systems. Such issues include but are not limited to the following:

- A large-scale network is required to market and deliver services effectively.

- Dormant PHOs are natural vehicles for assuming risk; however, many are specialist dominated and lack the capability to manage risk effectively.
- Relationships with existing individual practice associations (IPAs) in the market or relationships with strong PHOs and major IPAs need to be forged.
- Adverse selection appears likely.
- Strong resource management systems need to be implemented in order to mitigate risk.
- Effective marketing organizations are required to sell PSO health plans to individual Medicare patients.
- Cost structures in many integrated delivery systems are still too high, and any movement by Medicare toward capitation will force the issue.

Providers contemplating the development of a PSO must be realistic in assessing both the opportunities and potential drawbacks. The providers should view as a favorable sign an ability on their part to obtain a full risk contract for Medicare beneficiaries, which would represent initial business for the entity.

A PSO has the potential to serve alternative market segments while simultaneously preserving relationships with managed care organizations. If an integrated delivery system contracts directly with self-funded employers, the PSO could serve the employers' Medicare-eligible retirees. The PSO also has the potential to serve as a vehicle for converting into capitated revenue subsegments of the market not penetrated by managed care organizations.

The main object of forming a PSO can be either to convert Medicare payments into capitated revenue streams or to enter the Medicare risk contracting market while barriers are low. The PSO also can be used as a vehicle for gaining leverage with managed care organizations. Providers threatening forward integration—that is, threatening to form a PSO—could gain access to capitated contracts. Regardless of how significant the managed care organizations may view the PSO as being, they may conclude that negotiating concessions to providers is a less disruptive alternative than inviting competition. On the other hand, providers choosing not to form a PSO may also gain contracting leverage, since managed care organizations may offer favorable terms and substantial market share to substitute providers.

The Balanced Budget Act of 1997, which endorses the formation of PSOs, creates opportunities for providers to compete in the Medicare risk contracting market. These opportunities, however, if they are to be taken advantage of, require flexibility by providers. Competition is expected to grow, which is indeed the major goal of this piece of legislation. Providers must be able to comprehend the opportunities and threats within their own market. If they do not have a realistic assessment of their own strengths and weakness, then the likelihood that they will be able to successfully establish a PSO is not great.

NOTES

1. *Managed Care Week,* 2 February 1998.
2. NAIC, 1996. (www.naic.org)

CHAPTER 2

Provider Sponsored Organizations: Providers Searching for Opportunity

Bruce M. Fried and Janice H. Ziegler

A new era in the history of the Medicare Program opened with the enactment of the Balanced Budget Act of 1997 (BBA).[1] Specifically, through this act Congress created the new Medicare+Choice Program and authorized the secretary of Health and Human Services to enter, for the first time, into risk-based contracts with provider sponsored organizations (PSOs).[2] With this development comes new opportunities for providers to compete with managed care organizations—as well as new levels of confusion for Medicare beneficiaries, who are expected to choose among potentially numerous competing health care delivery systems. And, on a larger scale, new opportunities and risks confront the nation, the health care system, and individual citizens as the United States seeks to control health care spending while maintaining accessible high-quality health care.

This chapter explores the philosophical and political underpinnings of the new PSO option and provides an analysis of the legislative and regulatory policies that will shape this new delivery system. While much is known about the general framework in which PSOs will operate, there remain many issues yet to be clarified by the administration. Over the coming months, important regulations will be promulgated that will have a significant bearing on the composition, structure, and responsibilities of PSOs and the opportunities and challenges that they face.

PROVIDER SPONSORED ORGANIZATIONS: A NEW VINTAGE OR OLD WINE IN NEW BOTTLES?

As anyone who is involved in the health care system knows, the rate at which managed care has achieved dominance in the health care marketplace has been phenomenal. Less than 20 years ago, managed care was largely a West Coast phenomenon defined, for the most part, by nonprofit staff and group model health maintenance organizations (HMOs). Few outside the metropolitan areas of California, Oregon, Washington, and the New England area had any experience with integrated delivery systems reimbursed on a per capita basis. Today the vast majority of insured working persons and their dependents receive care through some sort of managed care organization. Better than 50 percent of Medicaid enrollees participate in a managed care organization, and the number of Medicare beneficiaries in managed care plans exceeds six million. The latter number has grown by approximately 90,000 beneficiaries each month for more than two years.

This dramatic change was brought about by the need of corporate health care purchasers and others to control the growth of health care spending. Beginning in the mid-eighties, private sector purchasers turned to market strategies to control costs, an objective that remained beyond the reach of governmental resolution, notwithstanding the efforts of virtually every president since Franklin Roosevelt. By creating incentives that rewarded control of the growth of health costs, private sector purchasers created a market where none existed before. Managed care organizations responded to those incentives. Thus far, the expanding managed care market has achieved enormous success in constraining the growth of health care costs for private purchasers.

The consequences of that success have been profound. Traditional centers of power in the health care system have seen their position erode as managed care organizations have become multi-billion dollar enterprises. The health care system, which not too many years ago was a cottage industry composed of independent community hospitals and free-standing private practitioners arranged in a desegregated, crazy-quilt "system," now finds itself in the throes of rampant aggregation and consolidation. Seeking to maximize both economic efficiency and bargaining power, hospitals, physicians, and other providers have joined together in both profit and nonprofit arrangements.

And yet even with this consolidation, hospitals and physicians often find themselves subordinate to managed care organizations, which contract with public and private purchasers and then subcontract with physicians and hospitals for the delivery of care and the bearing of risk. Beginning in the early 1990s, integrated delivery networks of hospitals and physicians began searching for opportunities to directly contract with purchasers on a risk basis. In some instances, integrated delivery networks chose to become HMOs and were able to be licensed as such by the states in which they operated. In other instances, integrated delivery networks found the licensing process too rigorous or the licensing agencies unable to recognize the distinction between provider-based networks and HMOs. Still other integrated delivery systems found themselves politically thwarted in their efforts to become licensed.

By the mid 1990s, trends began to converge, and the federal policy-making apparatus started considering ways in which new kinds of managed care organizations (including PSOs and preferred provider organizations [PPOs]) could contract with the government to provide services to Medicare beneficiaries. The Balanced Budget Act of 1995, which was not enacted, included significant provisions that would have allowed new contracting opportunities for these kinds of organizations. In the Balanced Budget Act of 1997, Congress included provisions that collectively are known as Medicare Part C. Among these provisions is one authorizing the Medicare+Choice program, which allows an array of new organizations to contract with the federal government in order to offer their services to the Medicare population. Beyond PSOs and PPOs, there are private fee-for-service insurers, Medical Savings Accounts (MSAs), and religious fraternal organizations. While some of the new arrangements were included in the legislation over the opposition of the administration, the PSO and PPO provisions enjoyed legislative and executive branch support.

THE OBJECTIVES OF THE MEDICARE+CHOICE PROGRAM

In enacting Medicare+Choice, the government had several objectives. First, policy makers intended to offer Medicare beneficiaries a wider array of choices than were previously available. In particular, the expectation was that PSOs and other new choices would extend to Medicare beneficiaries the array of choices available to many in the private sector. Beyond that, there was an expectation that in many parts of the country PSOs would develop where HMOs had not, thereby bringing the managed care option to many new Medicare beneficiaries.

Second, increasing the number and kinds of choices available to Medicare beneficiaries was expected to result in increased competition. The idea was that increased competition would not only reduce costs and improve benefits for beneficiaries (a phenomenon that had been observed in communities where more than three HMOs competed for the same Medicare business) but also set the stage for budgetary savings realized by the federal government.

Third, there was an expectation that allowing hospitals and physicians to combine to compete with established managed care organizations would "balance" the interests of these entities, restore greater local control to the management of health care, and put in charge of managed care decision-making clinicians and administrators closer to the patient and to the community.

The die is now cast. Whether these policy objectives will be achieved will depend on what occurs in local markets across the country.

PSO ALCHEMY

The legislative and regulatory policies that will define the structure, financing, and operations of PSOs are described below. Forming a PSO is a highly complicated and intensely regulated undertaking, and a decision to form one will need to be carefully considered. Beyond the structural and operational issues rest more fundamental and practical concerns: will the local market, the competitive environment, the economics of reimbursement rates, and the culture of the PSO lead to ultimate success or to a morass that will entangle all who become involved in it?

The fact of the matter is that there is unlikely to be any single "ideal" situation in which to launch a PSO. Being successful in a PSO endeavor is going to take a significant commitment of time, energy, and resources. And there are, of course, many factors that can contribute to that success.

The location where a PSO operates may be the most significant factor in determining success. Location will determine

- whether there are sufficient Medicare beneficiaries in the service area to generate a sufficient volume of potential members
- what the reimbursement rate will be
- how much managed care penetration exists
- what kind of competition the PSO will confront

Clearly, the more dispersed the Medicare population in a service area, the more difficult it will be for any managed care organization to efficiently deliver services to members. Notwithstanding the significant increase in the minimum reimbursement rate authorized by the BBA for Medicare+Choice organizations, in rural areas of the country where the Medicare population is sparse, there will simply never be the critical mass necessary to allow for an efficient delivery system. Depending on a PSO's location, its 1998 reimbursement rate may range from as low as $367 per member per month to more than $750 per member per month. Of course, there is typically a commensurate variance in health care costs. Be that as it may, a PSO will not be capable of moving from a very low reimbursed county to a very high reimbursed county. Still, at the business planning stage, Medicare+Choice reimbursement rates should influence the determination of the PSO's proper service area.

Location will also determine the degree of managed care penetration. There are counties, typically in the West and in southern Florida, where Medicare managed care penetration exceeds 50 percent. A PSO considering entering the Medicare business in one of these counties would want to devise a strategy for capturing market share before it acted. On the other hand, the Medicare penetration rate nationally is only 16 percent. In many communities across the country, few if any Medicare beneficiaries have chosen the managed care option (and of course many do not even have the possibility of so choosing). In any of these communities, a PSO with a respected local identity should find significant opportunities for enrollment.

In a community that has little, if any, managed care penetration, factors that may be at work include the delivery system costs and the Medicare reimbursement rates. No matter how respected the institution or how high the present density of Medicare beneficiaries, if the Medicare capitation rate is insufficient to permit the PSO to be a viable business endeavor, then there is no opportunity for success.

Of course, the capitation rate is one variable in a complex calculus that may be predictive of economic viability. Another key variable will be the organization's ability to manage risk. Indeed, next to location, risk management ability may be the most important factor determining the ultimate success or failure of a PSO. In truth, the capitation rate may actually be the only certain number in this complex calculus. Whether the PSO can meet its obligations to Medicare beneficiaries within the capitation rate will be determined by the cost of delivering care, the relative risk of the beneficiaries enrolling in the PSO, the cost of clinical and administrative services, and any number of other variables that deplete the funds received through capitation.

As administrators work to manage the PSO's risk, few tasks will be more difficult than modifying the organization's corporate culture. It is one thing for corporate risk managers in HMOs to manage care, but it is another for PSO administrators to manage their friends and colleagues. PSO managers and the PSO's board may find it difficult to impose discipline and incentive structures that have proven to be essential for success. Facing the hard realities of excess capacity, whether in facilities or medical personnel, making the difficult decisions that are inevitable, and communicating those decisions to colleagues and friends will be as challenging as anything else the PSO will undertake. Identifying clinicians who are outliers as regards practice patterns, exploring their practice variability, and bringing their practice patterns in line with more effective and efficient clinical approaches will be difficult as well. Yet without discipline and order, there is no management, and without management, economic efficiency and superior clinical performance cannot be achieved.

WHY WOULD PROVIDERS WANT TO FORM A PSO?

That's a fair question. The task of establishing a PSO will be worth the effort only if the opportunities the PSO structure presents are realized. For many providers, there has been a growing sense of loss of control in the health care experience. This loss of control evidences itself in the fundamental patient-physician relationship, clinical decision-making, and membership in health networks. Ownership of a PSO perhaps provides the best opportunity for hospitals and physicians to exercise control in these and other areas. The age of unmanaged health care is over. One way or another, whether at the local level and among peers or by managers of a corporate HMO, providers and physicians will either manage or be managed.

The flip side of opportunity, however, is liability. There will be little about the formation, management, or operation of the PSO that will be easy; but, then, little in medicine is these days. Perhaps the greatest drawback is potential failure. While there have been few managed care failures in recent years, as recently as the late eighties some two dozen provider-owned Medicare HMOs went under. Those failures, largely attributable to inexperience at managing risk for the Medicare population and insufficient resources to obtain the necessary experience, have largely shaped the policies that have since regulated the Medicare managed care program.

While Medicare regulations and policy have helped to ensure fiscal and managerial stability, the complicated regulatory environment[3] will make operating a PSO challenging. In the end, the viability of Medicare PSOs remains untested. The requirement that the providers in a PSO share, directly or indirectly, substantial financial risk and at least a majority financial interest in the PSO offers them an opportunity to share profits and burdens them with potential deficits. This is ultimately what risk is all about. The consequences of failure need to be carefully understood, and the place to begin developing such an understanding is with a careful analysis of the statutory and regulatory framework (as described below) and its implications for the providers and physicians that will make up the PSO entity.

The following pages discuss Medicare's traditional prepaid health plan options, the PSO provisions in the BBA and the more specific regulatory policies that are in the process of being developed. The standards and requirements that a PSO will have to meet in order to become a Medicare contractor are extensive and complex. Many who have thought of the formation of a PSO as a quick trip to the bank will see that it is unlikely to be a means of obtaining easy money. Nonetheless, this new type of Medicare managed care organization will offer important new opportunities for Medicare beneficiaries, the communities they live in, and the providers who serve them.

The future of the Medicare program, as well as the future of the nation's health care system, lies in value-based health care. A value-based system is one that strives for the highest quality of care at the lowest justifiable price. Given the realities of the demographics of the United States and the current economic constraints of families, businesses, and all levels of government, a health care system that consumes one-seventh of the gross domestic product cannot function without sensitive management. Managed care is here to stay, and PSOs will be a critical part of the managed care sector.

THE HISTORY OF MEDICARE'S PREPAID HEALTH CARE PROGRAM

Prepaid "managed care" health plans have been part of Medicare since the program's inception in 1965. These early Medicare managed care plans were little more than experiments in alternative reimbursement methodologies. Few organizations sought to participate in the demonstration program, even with the availability of what was essentially venture capital in the form of federal loans to provide initial capitalization. The Tax Equity and Fiscal Responsibility Act of 1982 (TEFRA) established the structure for the Medicare managed care program as it exists today. Most important was the risk-contracting program,[4] which authorized the secretary of Health and Human Services to enter into contracts with state licensed managed care organizations that met certain TEFRA standards and could provide the Medicare program's benefits to those enrolled in a particular plan. It has been the risk program that has grown the most dramatically, in terms of the numbers of beneficiaries enrolled in risk-based plans and the number of contracts being entered into by the secretary.

Features of TEFRA HMOs and CMPs

To date, alternatives to Medicare's fee-for-service program have been limited to state licensed HMOs and comprehensive medical plans (CMPs) that meet the standards set forth in TEFRA.[5] Understanding these standards is important, since they will in most instances apply to Medicare+Choice plans, including PSOs. The standards are designed to ensure managerial and fiscal stability, comprehensiveness of the medical delivery system, access to and quality of care, and patient protection.

The Ability To Bear Risk

The secretary is given the discretion to determine if an entity seeking a Medicare risk contract has the capacity to bear risk, that is, to be prepaid on a capitated basis and meet all enrollee health care needs and other plan obligations. Demonstrating the ability to bear risk typically requires, in addition to being able to manage risk, being licensed by the state or states in which the plan operates and meeting state fiscal solvency standards.[6]

Managerial and Administrative Capacity

Plans must be able to adequately manage and administer their business and meet the regulatory, contractual, and operational requirements of the Medicare program. No person who has been convicted of a crime involving Medicare or Medicaid may be an owner, manager, or agent of a Medicare HMO or CMP (or, in all likelihood, a PSO).

Minimum Enrollment and Composition

The TEFRA HMO-CMP standards require that health plans in rural areas have at least 1,500 capitated members and health plans in areas other than rural have at least 5,000 capitated members. TEFRA also requires, in the so-called 50/50 rule, that at least 50 percent of a plan's enrollees be neither Medicare nor Medicaid eligible. (The BBA eliminates the 50/50 rule, and for PSOs sets a different standard for minimum enrollment. See below.)

Health Care Delivery

The plan must be able to directly or indirectly (through contracting) deliver the full range of Medicare required services to the enrollees within the plan's service area. Such services must be provided through Medicare-certified providers. The plan may not use providers that have been excluded from participation in the Medicare program.

Services To Be Provided

HMOs and CMPs must provide all services covered by Part A and Part B of Medicare to Medicare beneficiaries enrolled in the plan. In addition to the standard Medicare benefits, plans can offer additional benefits (these result when the adjusted community rate [ACR] exceeds the payment rate, in which case the plan must either return the difference to the U.S. Treasury or offer it to beneficiaries in terms of reduced premiums or improved benefits), optional supplemental benefits (which any beneficiary may purchase), and mandatory supplemental benefits (which all beneficiaries enrolling in the plan may be required to purchase).[7]

Open Enrollment

Generally, HMOs and CMPs must be open to enrollment during at least one 30-day period each year. In practice, the vast majority of Medicare plans are continuously open to new enrollment. The statute does not allow individuals with end-stage renal disease (ESRD) to enroll in a plan unless their illness occurred when they were already enrolled. Similarly, hospice patients may not enroll in an HMO or a CMP.

Marketing

Medicare plans are required to market their services throughout the service area and may not exclude any group of Medicare eligibles from their marketing effort. All marketing materials targeted to Medicare beneficiaries, both print and electronic, must be submitted to the Health Care Financing Administration (HCFA) for review. If HCFA takes no action within 45 days, the materials are deemed approved. Certain marketing activities are prohibited, including door-to-door soliciting, discriminatory marketing, and misrepresentation. HCFA published Medicare Managed Care National Marketing Guidelines in 1997 to provide additional guidance in this complex area. The guidelines are available from HCFA or may be found at HCFA's Internet site (www.hcfa.gov/Medicare/market.htm).

Quality Assurance

Both HMOs and CMPs must have quality assurance (QA) programs in place to make certain that high-quality health care is being delivered to patients. These programs must address outcomes of care and peer review, collect and analyze data for the purpose of improving the quality of care, and develop a strategy for making necessary improvements to care delivery.

The Contracting Process

Managed care organizations desiring to contract with HCFA may obtain the contract application and supporting materials from HCFA's Center for Health Plans and Providers. Currently, applications are available for HMOs and CMPs.[8] The application is comprehensive and complex. It requires the applicant to specify the area that will be served, the benefits that will be provided, the organization's marketing strategy, specific information regarding providers and clinicians in its health services delivery system, evidence of coverage (including membership rules), employee rights and plan benefits, details regarding the organization's quality assurance plan, the processes for enrollment and disenrollment, and the plan's grievance and appeals procedures. The application also requires submission of information regarding the nature of the applicant's organization, its executive officers and board, its management capability, and its fiscal solvency and financial management.

It is not unusual for a managed care application to take as much as six months to prepare. Once an application is submitted, HCFA's staff conducts a preliminary review to verify the completeness of the application. If the application is determined to be incomplete as originally submitted, the applicant is allowed not more than 60 days to perfect the application. Applications that remain incomplete after 60 days are deemed to have been withdrawn.

If the application is complete, it receives an intense review by HCFA staff, both at its central office and in the field. The review is both a desk review (where written submissions are scrutinized for compliance with the relevant standards) and a field review (where an on-site examination is conducted that focuses on all aspects of the applicant's submission).

Generally, HCFA attempts to complete review of an application and enter into a contract (where appropriate) within a six-month period, though there is no requirement that applications be processed within that time frame. Indeed, there have been periods where HCFA has taken significantly longer to process applications. Typically this occurs when the volume of applications exceeds the resources of the agency to process them in a timely manner.

Once HCFA has determined that an applicant meets all relevant standards, a contract is entered into between the applicant and HCFA, acting on behalf of the United States of America. Contracts are automatically renewed with effective dates of January 1 of each succeeding year.

The Adjusted Average per Capita Cost and Other Historic Payment Schemes

TEFRA authorized the secretary of Health and Human Services to enter into three kinds of contracts or arrangements with eligible health plans: risk contracts, cost contracts, and health care prepaid plan (HCPP) arrangements. Health plans with risk contracts received payments based on a complex formula known as the adjusted average per capita cost (AAPCC). Each year HCFA would calculate the average cost of providing Part A (inpatient care) and Part B (physician and outpatient care) services to Medicare beneficiaries in each county in the nation. A risk contractor would receive 95 percent of the AAPCC for each beneficiary that enrolled in its plan.[9] The plan would then be fully at risk to provide all of the Medicare-covered benefits to its enrollees. Under cost contracts, plans received a capitated payment based on projected costs of care for enrollees. At the end of each year, the plans would reconcile the payments they received with the actual costs of care, and appropriate payments would be made or received. Finally, HCPPs received a capitated payment for Medicare Part B services and fee-for-services reimbursement for Part A services.

The BBA directs that no new cost contracts be entered into after the date of enactment and that current cost contracts not be renewed beyond December 31, 2002.

THE MEDICARE MANAGED CARE EXPERIENCE: EARLY FAILURES, RECENT GROWTH

With TEFRA's new managed care provisions, the Medicare managed care program began to grow—slowly in terms of beneficiaries but quickly in terms of the number of contracts. By 1988, the secretary had entered into some 125 TEFRA prepaid contracts. Importantly, in the late 1980s, some two dozen of the early Medicare HMOs failed. Generally, as noted above, these failures were a consequence of lack of experience in managing care for the Medicare population,[10] the administrative challenge of meeting Medicare regulatory and program requirements, and insufficient capitalization to obtain the needed experience.

Some plans failed but others succeeded. By the mid-1990s, the number of Medicare plans began to grow rapidly, and the number of Medicare beneficiaries opting for the managed care option followed. Over the past three years, the rate of growth in the number of beneficiaries enrolling in managed care has held steady at about two percent per month. The continued rapid rate of growth in Medicare managed care plans is a function of the economic benefits that many managed care plans have offered (zero or reduced premiums and better benefits than the traditional Medicare program) as well as the fact that many employers are now offering Medicare HMOs as the means by which they will provide ongoing retiree health care benefits. By January 1998, more than six million beneficiaries were in managed care plans (5.3 million of them in risk contracts), approximately 16 percent of all Medicare enrollees. Managed care plan enrollees were concentrated in metropolitan areas. At the same time, there were more than 440 contracts with managed care plans of all types, with approximately 50 applications pending consideration at HCFA.

The BBA brought about a significant change in the enrollment process for Medicare+Choice plans. That new process, which is described below, may dramatically increase enrollment. The process includes an annual public education program, to be conducted in November of each year, with a coordinated open enrollment process. Many observers believe that this may be viewed by beneficiaries as an implicit endorsement of Medicare health plans, thus reducing the fear and apprehension that have kept many beneficiaries from enrolling in Medicare managed care organizations.

Whether the government has saved money or controlled expenditures as a result of managed care is a matter of some debate. Any number of studies, both by private and public researchers, have concluded that the government is actually paying as much as five percent more for patients in managed care than is justified. Underlying this conclusion is the fact that while the AAPCC payment scheme paid 95 percent of the fee-for-service cost for the average beneficiary in a particular county, the beneficiaries enrolling in managed care have been on average healthier and therefore less costly to serve than the Medicare population in general. Some researchers have noted that this "favorable selection" phenomenon will decrease as managed care captures larger shares of the health care market and the average managed care enrollee becomes more representative. Others assert that favorable selection will persist given the economic incentives of the AAPCC, the inherent preference that managed care has for the less risky patient, and other demographic factors. All that taken into consideration, controlling health care expenditures, which appears to be the holy grail of health care policy during the baby-boomer onslaught, will require a more organized, more managed, more integrated health care system than that which has existed previously or that which exists today.

BEYOND TEFRA: THE PUSH FOR GREATER CHOICE

From the mid-1980s to the mid-1990s, Medicare's managed care options were limited to HMOs and CMPs, both state licensed insurance entities. While both group and staff model and independent practice association model HMOs became available to Medicare beneficiaries in many parts of the country, the managed care option remained out of reach for those outside of traditional managed care strongholds. Thus, as noted above, until the mid-1990s most beneficiaries in managed care resided in California, the Southwest, and southern Florida. This fact was a consequence not only of the historical development of managed care but also of the wide variance in reimbursement rates. In 1997, some urban areas were receiving AAPCC payments in excess of $750 per member per month whereas some rural counties received less than $250. Clearly, there was little incentive for health plans to develop in counties with relatively low payments until high payment counties were fully penetrated.

Not only was the availability of Medicare managed care geographically limited, but the types of managed care available to Medicare beneficiaries were not keeping pace with developments in the private sector. Managed care arrangements proliferated as health plans tested new delivery structures, risk-sharing arrangements, and more loosely managed schemes in the quest for greater market share and product differentiation. Preferred provider organizations, point-of-service models, and other variations of managed care became the dominant models offered by private sector companies to their employees and dependents. For many health care policy and political leaders, expanding choice for Medicare beneficiaries became an imperative.

As the managed care industry was developing new models, health care providers were struggling to gain a foothold in the health care market. Hospitals, physicians, and others consolidated and integrated, initially to be more economically efficient. A consequence was that the initial ability of health plans to squeeze savings out of disaggregated, uncoordinated, and inefficient providers began to fade. Integrated delivery systems found more strength in their relations with managed care plans. Indeed, large integrated systems, physician management groups, and individual practice associations (IPAs) began to question why they should not simply bypass managed care plans and seek direct contracts with public and private purchasers of care. Hospitals, physicians, integrated delivery networks, and others pursued a political strategy to enter Medicare risk arrangements. From that effort was born Medicare+Choice.

MEDICARE+CHOICE: THE MEDICARE PROGRAM OF THE FUTURE

Section 4001 of the BBA creates a new Medicare Part C Program and, in so doing, fundamentally changes the Medicare program (though generally building on the delivery system options, payment methodologies, enrollment processes, member composition and other aspects of the TEFRA Medicare managed care program).

The act expands the types of capitated plans available to beneficiaries.[11] As implementation unfolds in 1999, the act will allow a broader range of plans to participate in Medicare on a capitated basis, a range comparable to what is now available in the private sector.

Coordinated Care Plans

Coordinated care plans (CCPs) include HMOs, PSOs, PPOs, religious fraternal benefit plans, and other coordinated care plans that meet the Medicare+Choice standards.

Private Fee-for-Service Plans

The BBA defines private fee-for-service (PFFS) plans as those plans that cover services from any qualified provider and pay physicians on a fee-for-service basis. These plans may not have utilization-based bonuses or penalties or otherwise place providers at financial risk.

Medical Savings Accounts—High Deductible Plans

MSAs are only available to certain individuals in the context of a nationwide demonstration limited to an enrollment of 390,000 beneficiaries for the years 1999–2002. Like PFFS plans, MSAs cover services from any qualified provider and pay physicians on a fee-for-service basis, with no utilization-based bonuses or penalties. An MSA must cover at least those services covered by Medicare's traditional fee-for-service plan, but only after an enrollee incurs countable expenses equal to the amount of an annual deductible.[12] Once such a deductible is met, the MSA may (but need not) cover all incurred expenses. (The BBA requires only that MSAs pay the lesser of all costs incurred or all costs that would have been allowable in Medicare's fee-for-service sector.)

Despite the nomenclature, MSAs need not actually be high deductible plans, since the BBA specifies a maximum MSA deductible (equal to $6,000 in 1999) rather than a minimum. MSA enrollees are required to establish a medical savings account, into which any excess of the Medicare annual capitation payment amount over the plan's premium is deposited. MSA enrollees may use the funds in their accounts to pay their out-of-pocket medical expenses, although there is no guarantee that those funds will be sufficient.

While much can and will be written on all of these new choices, this discussion will focus on the implications of the BBA for PSOs.

SO, WHAT IS A PSO?

The BBA provides some guidance on the definition of a PSO. Moreover, other aspects of the definition were recently illuminated in regulations issued by the Secretary of Health and Human Services.[13]

A PSO is a public or private entity established or organized and operated by a health care provider or a group of affiliated providers that provide a substantial proportion of the health care items and services under the Medicare+Choice[14] contract directly through the provider or the affiliated group of providers.[15] Affiliated providers share, directly or indirectly, substantial financial risk[16] for the provision of items and services under the Medicare contract between the government and the PSO and have at least a majority financial interest in the PSO.[17] A "substantial proportion" of health care items or services has been defined by regulation as 70 percent of the value of the Medicare basic benefit package for non-rural PSOs and 60 percent for rural PSOs. By requiring that a substantial proportion of services be provided directly by the PSO's providers, Congress has essentially required that the PSO include both hospitals and physicians. (It is difficult to see how physicians or hospitals alone could meet the substantial proportion test.) Providers would be "affiliated" if, through contract, ownership, or otherwise (1) one provider was, directly or indirectly, controlled by or under common control of the other;[18] (2) each provider is a participant in a lawful combination under which he or she shares "substantial financial risk" in connection with the PSO's operations; (3) both or all providers are part of a "controlled group" of corporations per Section 1563 of the Internal Revenue Code (IRC); or (4) both providers are part of an "affiliated service" under Section 414 of the IRC.

Licensure

Under certain circumstances, PSOs may be able to enter into Medicare+Choice contracts without state licenses, but this unusual waiver of state insurance regulation will only exist for the next several years.[19] Waiver requests must be filed by November 1, 2002.[20] HCFA may waive the state licensure requirement if the organization has applied for the most closely appropriate state license or authority to conduct business as a Medicare+Choice plan and any of the following conditions apply: (1) the state failed to process the PSO's application within 90 days after a substantially completed application was filed; (2) the state acted discriminatorily by denying the application on the basis of requirements or standards not generally applicable to other entities in substantially the same business or by conditioning licensure on the PSO's offering any product or plan other than a Medicare+Choice plan; (3) the state PSO solvency standards were not the same as the federal standards (see discussion below); or (4) the state licensing authority has notified the organization in writing that it will not accept their licensure application.[21] The secretary is required to grant or deny a federal waiver request within 60 days after a "substantially completed" request is filed. All state standards that are not inconsistent with federal law will remain in force. Waivers will be effective for 36 months and may not be renewed.

As this chapter is being written, HCFA is in the process of finalizing comprehensive Medicare+Choice regulations. Until they are published, we must look to the statute for guidance concerning benefits and other matters discussed below.

Benefits

PSOs must cover at least the same services as are covered in the Medicare fee-for-service program. PSOs may offer mandatory and optional supplemental benefits (consistent with the ACR process), and plan premiums for required benefits may not exceed the cost-sharing expenses beneficiaries would face in the fee-for-service sector.

Beneficiary Protections

The standards regarding information disclosure, access to care, quality, grievances and appeals, confidentiality, and information on advance directives are similar to those required by TEFRA. The Medicare+Choice regulations will detail these requirements.

Disclosure

PSOs must provide to each enrollee in a clear, accurate, and standardized form, certain information, including a description of the plan's service area; the benefits offered; the number, mix, and distribution of providers; conditions regarding out-of-area and emergency coverage; the scope of any supplemental benefits; preauthorization rules; processes for appeals and grievances; and the quality assurance program.

Access

PSOs may select the providers who may furnish benefits to enrollees. Covered benefits must be available and accessible to all enrollees as medically necessary with reasonable promptness and assured continuity 24 hours a day, seven days a week. Emergency services must be provided without regard to prior authorization or whether the provider is part of the PSO's delivery system.

Quality Assurance

PSOs must have an internal QA program and undergo external quality reviews by a peer review organization (PRO) or an independent review organization. Internal QA requirements could be met by receiving accreditation from a private organization approved by the secretary. External review could be waived for PSOs with a good track record.[22] These QA requirements build on quality standards under TEFRA.

In addition to these provisions, HCFA is engaged in a major expansion of its efforts to capture quality performance data from Medicare managed care plans. Beginning in 1997 and annually thereafter, HCFA will require all Medicare managed care organizations to collect and report Medicare relevant data from the Health Employer Data and Information Set (HEDIS). (HEDIS is a set of performance measures developed by the National Committee for Quality Assurance.) Additionally, HCFA will begin surveying a statistically valid sample of beneficiaries enrolled in every Medicare managed care organization beginning in 1998 and annually thereafter to gauge their experience in receiving care from their health plans. This survey will employ the Consumer Assessment Health Plan Satisfaction (CAHPS) survey tool, which measures the patient's experience in terms of quality, access, and overall satisfaction. Using these and other quality performance indicators, HCFA will begin to assess and compare the performance of managed care organizations.

Appeals and Grievances

PSOs are required to have and maintain meaningful, timely procedures for resolving disputes over medical services or claims. Thus, PSOs will be required to have an expedited appeals process in cases where the normal time frame for making a determination on reconsideration could seriously jeopardize the life or health of an enrollee or the enrollee's ability to regain maximum function. Requests for expedited review made by a physician must be granted. Expedited determinations must be made within a time frame appropriate to the medical situation but not later than 72 hours after the request for expedited review. Appeals from decisions unfavorable to the enrollee will be adjudicated by an independent entity. If that entity's decision is unfavorable to the beneficiary, then further appeals can be pursued with an administrative law judge, the department appeals board, and the federal courts. Nonexpedited decisions at present must be made within 60 days. The regulations will, however, in all likelihood significantly reduce that time period to either 10 working days or 14 calendar days. In any event, PSOs will be required to have a grievance process in place to handle enrollee complaints regarding anything other than disputes over medical services or claims.

Confidentiality

The BBA requires Medicare+Choice organizations to establish procedures to safeguard the privacy of enrollee information and to ensure that Medicare enrollees have access to their individual records.

Antidiscrimination Protections

Medicare+Choice organizations are prohibited from denying, limiting, or conditioning the coverage or provision of benefits based on a beneficiary's health status. (The one exception is for individuals with ESRD, who are precluded from enrolling in a Medicare+Choice organization after having been so diagnosed.) Additionally, the BBA prohibits Medicare+Choice organizations from discriminating against any provider who is acting within the scope of his or her license.[23]

Modification of TEFRA Standards

The BBA, which generally incorporates the TEFRA standards, modifies those standards in two important respects. To begin, as of 1999 (with waivers available earlier), the requirement that at least half of each plan's enrollment must be commercial will no longer apply. The 50/50 rule was originally intended as a surrogate to ensure the quality of the risk-based plans serving Medicare beneficiaries. Since the act mandates heightened QA devices, the rule was no longer viewed as necessary. In any event, the 50/50 rule was seen as creating an unfortunate and unnecessary ceiling to enrollment in risk-based plans, particularly in rural areas.

Moreover, for PSOs only, the BBA reduced the minimum enrollment requirements imposed. Thus, PSOs in rural areas will be required to bear risk for at least 500 enrollees, and in all other areas they must bear risk for at least 1,500 enrollees. The act permits waivers for all plans, but it is unlikely that HCFA will allow a plan to have less than 500 enrollees.

The Contracting Process

Upon the issuance of the state license or a federal waiver, the PSO may apply to HCFA for certification and a federal contract.

It is anticipated that the application process will be similar to the present Medicare risk CMP application process. Core PSO applications are presently available and being accepted for processing by HCFA for state-licensed PSOs. Once the comprehensive Medicare+Choice regulations are issued, the agency anticipates releasing a supplemental PSO application form to be completed by all PSOs that have previously submitted a core PSO application. It is further anticipated that in 1999 and thereafter, PSOs will only need to complete one comprehensive form. The PSO certification process will require a showing of compliance with applicable federal standards and will include a site visit by HCFA officials.

Payments to Medicare+Choice Plans

The BBA changed the way in which Medicare's payment rates are calculated for Medicare+Choice plans, including PSOs.[24] In general, beginning in 1998, Medicare capitation rates paid to plans will be the greater of (1) a minimum payment amount, to be updated annually by growth in Medicare fee-for-service costs minus 0.8 percent in 1998 and minus 0.5 percent thereafter[25]; (2) a minimum percentage increase from, for most areas, the 1997 AAPCC rate; or (3) a blend of the area-specific rate (updated annually) and an input-price adjusted national rate, further modified by budget neutrality adjustments.[26] Due to the budget neutrality requirements, in 1998 no county will receive the blended rate (and this probably will be the case for several more years). Rates for each calendar year are announced by March 1 of the preceding year. The update factor for the minimum payment rate and the area-specific rate used in the blended rate will be the national average per capita Medicare growth rate, reduced by 0.5 percent in 1999 through 2002. Beyond 2002, there is no reduction.

In order to have more individually sensitive payments to plans, including PSOs, the BBA directs the secretary to propose by March 1, 1999, a method to adjust plan payments to reflect the relative risk of each enrollee. To allow risk-adjusted payments, PSOs and other Medicare+Choice plans will be required to capture and report data on inpatient and other "encounters." The new risk-adjusted payment plan is to begin on January 1, 2000.

Setting Premiums and Benefits: The ACR Process

The methodology for setting Medicare+Choice plan premiums and mandatory and supplemental benefits is essentially the same as set out in TEFRA. The ACR process is the means by which plans set premiums and benefits that will be offered to beneficiaries. Historically it has allowed TEFRA risk contractors to offer zero premium plans, drug benefits, dental and hearing care, and other benefits not covered by the traditional Medicare program. These added benefits and reduced costs have provided incentives for many economically sensitive consumers to opt for managed care.

The process begins on March 1 of each year with the announcement by HCFA's Office of the Actuary of the payment rates for each county in the nation. (Any changes in the methodology or assumptions used to calculate the rates must be announced at least 45 days prior to March 1.) By May 1 of each year, PSOs and other managed care plans must submit to the secretary ACR proposals for basic and supplemental benefits, the premium for the basic and supplemental benefits, a description of cost sharing and the actuarial value of cost sharing for basic and supplemental benefits, and a description of any additional benefits and the value of those benefits. The ACR is the rate that reflects the projected actual cost of delivering the basic Medicare benefits. As previously noted, the difference between the capitated amount that will be paid to the plans and the ACR amount must be either returned to the United States Treasury or provided to enrolled beneficiaries through reduced premiums and increased benefits.

The ACR submission is reviewed by HCFA's central and regional office staff for accuracy and compliance with the process. While it is currently a paper process, the agency is developing a mechanism for electronic submission. Once the ACR receives approval, the plan is obligated to offer at least the approved premiums, benefits, and other plan options to its enrollees (for example, a point-of-service option might be offered). During the course of the contract year, the deal for beneficiaries can never be diminished, though plans often improve premium or benefit offerings in response to market competition.

The premium and benefit arrangements for all plans will need to be finally approved by HCFA by late summer in order for HCFA to accurately describe the details of each plan's program during the public information campaign that will be conducted annually each November. ACR-approved benefits and premiums are effective for each contract year and may be altered only during the next ACR process.

Any premiums charged by Medicare+Choice plans must be community rated and may not vary among plan enrollees.

Enrollment

The BBA will significantly alter the enrollment process for the Medicare risk-based plans in two primary respects.[27] First, it will mandate an annual coordinated election period designed to disseminate a broad range of information to Medicare beneficiaries for review and comparison prior to decision-making. Accordingly, under the BBA all Medicare+Choice plans will hold open enrollment during November of each year, beginning in 1999 for enrollment during 2000.[28] In advance of the open enrollment period, the secretary of Health and Human Services will be required to mail each Medicare beneficiary notice of the upcoming open enrollment, general information about Medicare, and comparative information about the Medicare+Choice plans available in the beneficiary's area. (Currently, no such process exists and there is no single source of such information.) The governmental notice will include general Medicare information concerning benefits, cost-sharing requirements, and balance billing liability under the original fee-for-service program as well as information concerning election procedures and Medigap and Medicare SELECT coverage options. Comparative information shall include extensive information concerning benefits and beneficiary liability, premiums, service areas, quality and performance, and supplemental benefits. The BBA requires that these efforts be supported by a toll-free number for inquiries concerning Medicare+Choice options and an Internet site[29] designed to provide additional helpful information.[30]

Second, the BBA will limit the enrollees' current virtually unfettered ability to switch plans or to return to Medicare's fee-for-service sector during the year. Until the year 2002, Medicare beneficiaries will be able to disenroll from risk-based plans at any time (monthly) and either switch to another HMO (if one is open) or return to the fee-for-service sector simply by filling out an appropriate election form. In 2002, enrollees electing a Medicare+Choice plan will be allowed to change plans only once (apart from the annual open enrollment period) during the first six months of the year. In all subsequent years, they will be able to make only one change (apart from those made during the open enrollment period) during the first three months of the year. A newly eligible Medicare enrollee would still be allowed to disenroll from the fee-for-service program any time within his or her first 12 months of enrollment.

Marketing Materials

The marketing requirements of TEFRA prohibit health plans from distributing marketing materials unless they have been submitted to HCFA at least 45 days before the date of distribution and HCFA has not disapproved the materials. It is expected that the national marketing guidelines discussed earlier in this chapter will be applied to PSOs. The BBA flatly prohibits certain marketing practices, including cash rebates as an inducement for enrollment and a Medicare+Choice organization's completing any portion of any form used to select a health plan on behalf of a beneficiary.[31]

FISCAL SOLVENCY: PUT UP OR SHUT UP?

To make certain that PSOs have the financial resources to weather the inherent uncertainty of being at risk in a volatile market, the BBA included directions to the secretary regarding PSO solvency standards.[32] Clearly, the government must ensure that it will not be left holding the bag for PSOs (or, for that matter, any risk-bearing organization) should they fail. Otherwise, taxpayers, beneficiaries, and contracted providers would be subject to an unacceptable level of vulnerability.

Congress directed the secretary to develop final regulations setting forth solvency standards for PSOs through expedited negotiated rule-making.[33] Negotiated rule-making is a process established by Congress to engage parties with an interest in a particular issue in the development of the regulations that will set policy for that issue. In the case of PSO solvency standards, not only did Congress invoke the negotiated rule making process but it directed that the process be expedited so that an interim final regulation would be issued within a time period that would allow PSOs to complete the application process and begin Medicare operations early in 1999. Beginning with its first meeting on October 20, 1997, a committee of interested parties met to explore issues relevant to establishing the solvency standards and to reach a consensus on standards.[34] The BBA required the secretary and the committee, in developing the PSO standards, to take into account (1) the delivery system's assets and the PSO's ability to provide services directly, (2) alternative means of protecting against insolvency, and (3) standards developed by the National Association of Insurance Commissioners (NAIC) specifically for risk-based delivery organizations.

The work of the rule-making committee is reflected in the insolvency regulations published in May 1998.[35]

Net Worth

At the point of application, a PSO will generally be required to have a net worth of at least $1.5 million.[36] At least half of that amount will need to be in cash or cash equivalents. In considering assets that contribute to meeting the noncash portion of the net worth standard, 100 percent of the book value (i.e., Generally Accepted Accounting Principles [GAAP] depreciated value) of the PSO's health care delivery assets appearing on the balance sheet of the PSO or the legal entity of which the PSO applicant is a line of business could be admitted. These assets include hospitals, medical facilities and their ancillary equipment, and such property as may reasonably be required for the PSO's principal offices or for the transaction of the PSO's business. HCFA will request public comment on whether to use and/or modify Statutory Accounting Practices (SAP) codification standards on asset concentration and quality of health care delivery assets for waivered PSOs. Meanwhile, HCFA will apply its judgment in evaluating health care delivery assets for concentration and quality.

On an ongoing basis, PSOs will need to maintain a minimum net worth equal to the greater of (1) $1 million, (2) 2 percent of annual premium revenues as reported on the most recent annual financial statement filed with HCFA on the first $150,000,000 of annual premiums and 1 percent of annual premium revenues on the premiums in excess of $150,000,000, (3) an amount equal to the sum of three months uncovered health care expenditures as reported on the most recent financial statement filed with HCFA, or (4) 8 percent of annual health care expenditures paid on a non-capitated basis to non-affiliated providers as reported to HCFA plus 4 percent of annual health care expenditures paid on a capitated basis to non-affiliated providers and on a non-capitated basis to affiliated providers (regardless of downstream arrangements from affiliated providers).

A major item for consideration by the committee was the valuation of intangible assets, such as goodwill, and the percentage of the minimum net worth that such intangible assets could represent.[37] The following accord is reflected in the regulations: (1) if at least $1 million of the initial minimum net worth is met by cash or cash equivalents, then HCFA will admit the GAAP value of intangible assets up to 20 percent of the minimum net worth required, and (2) if less than $1 million of the initial minimum net worth requirement is met by cash or cash equivalents, or HCFA has used its discretion to reduce the initial net worth requirement below $1.5 million, then HCFA will admit the GAAP value of intangible assets up to 10 percent of the minimum net worth amount required. Slightly different rules will apply on a going forward basis.[38] If, once the three-year waiver period ends, the PSO intends to continue to contract with Medicare, it must demonstrate, through the required financial plan, how it will comply with state minimum net worth requirements under state standards for admitting intangible assets at the end of the three-year waiver period.

Financial Plan

At the outset, all PSOs will be required to submit financial plans covering the first 12 months of operation under the contract or if the PSO is projecting losses, 12 months beyond the period for which losses are projected. These plans must include a detailed marketing plan, statements of revenue and expense on an accrual basis, a cash flow statement, balance sheets, and the assumptions in support of the financial plan.

In the financial plan, the PSO must demonstrate that it has the resources available to meet all of the projected losses for the entire period to the break-even point. Except in limited circumstances, those resources must be in the form of cash or assets that can be converted into cash in a timely manner.[39]

Liquidity

This standard will basically require PSOs to have sufficient cash flow to meet their financial obligations as they become due. In determining whether a PSO meets this requirement, HCFA will examine a number of factors including the PSO's timeliness in meeting current obligations, the availability of outside financial resources to the PSO, and the extent to which the PSO's current ratio of assets to liabilities is maintained at 1:1 (and any declining trend in the ratio over time). If HCFA determines that a PSO fails to meet any of these criteria, it will require the PSO to initiate appropriate corrective action.

Insolvency

The solvency standard is intended to provide safeguards in the event that the PSO becomes insolvent. At the time of application, an organization must deposit $100,000 in case or securities in an account to help assume continuation of services or pay a liquidator's costs in the event of insolvency. These funds would count toward the required net worth. Additional monies would be required to be available in certain instances to pay for uncovered expenditures. In the event of insolvency, the PSO would likely be required to ensure that all beneficiary protections are maintained.[40]

Rural Providers

In recognizing the unique need of rural communities, the committee statement requests HCFA to solicit public comment for the purpose of determining whether downward adjustments to the net worth and liquidity requirements set forth in the statement are appropriate for rural providers.

CONCLUSION

PSOs offer providers new opportunities to regain power and control within the increasingly complex and competitive health care environment but not without risk. Wisdom, location, persistence, and, to some extent, luck will dictate the success of these ventures. Careful advance analysis of the potential benefits and legislative and regulatory burdens of offering services through these organizations will increase the ultimate chances of success.

NOTES

1. Public Law 105-33, 111 Stat. 251 (Aug. 5, 1997).
2. The Medicare+Choice program (i.e., Medicare Part C) is set forth in sections 1851–1857 and 1859 of the Social Security Act.
3. The risk-based Medicare managed care regime is a complicated one. For guidance, the relevant provisions of the Social Security Act, Health Care Financing Administration (HCFA) regulations, and any relevant operation policy letters should always be consulted. In addition, a wealth of information is available through the HCFA Internet web site (www.hcfa.gov). HCFA is the agency that administers Medicare.
4. TEFRA authorized risk contracts, cost contracts and contracts with health care prepaid plans (HCPPs). Public Law 97-248, 96 Stat. 324 (Sept. 3, 1982).
5. In addition to the statutory provisions found in section 1876 (42 USC §1395mm), Medicare managed care policies are also set out in a variety of regulations, including 42 CFR Part 422 et seq. Additional policy guidance is issued by HCFA through operation policy letters from HCFA's Center for Health Plans and Providers. Operation policy letters can also be found on HCFA's Internet site.
6. HCFA will soon promulgate new minimum standards, both fiscal and operational, for PSOs. The following discussion is based on what is known presently about what those standards will likely provide. An organization seeking a PSO contract will need to convince HCFA that it has a strong knowledge base and management capacity. The fact that a group of organizations has made an economic investment in the formation of a PSO will not alone be sufficient to gain a Medicare contract.
7. Indeed, this is what makes these plans so attractive to Medicare beneficiaries. By yielding some of their choice under the fee-for-service program, they can expand their benefits and/or reduce their Medicare deductible and coinsurance payments. As these risk-based plans proliferate in number and type and the network of providers participating in such plans expand, coordinated care plans (CCPs) will become even more attractive to seniors.
8. Core application materials for state-licensed PSOs are available from HCFA's Internet site.
9. Adjustments to those payments would be made to reflect the special status of some beneficiaries, including those over age 85, those with ESRD, those dually eligible for both Medicare and Medicaid, and the working aged.
10. As a general rule, Medicare beneficiaries consume four times more medical services than the commercial population.

11. Only Medicare beneficiaries entitled to Part A and enrolled in Part B are eligible to enroll in these plans, because capitation rates are based on the provision of Part A and Part B services. Even in this context, beneficiaries with ESRD may not enroll in Medicare+Choice plans but may remain in such plans if already enrolled at the onset of the disease.
12. The MSA must count as such expenses all amounts that would have been payable under Parts A and B and that would have been payable by the enrollee as deductibles, coinsurance, or copayments if the enrollee had elected to receive benefits through the provisions of such parts. Plans may include other countable expenses at their option.
13. 42 CFR §422.350 through 42 CFR § 422.356.
14. Generally, a Medicare+Choice organization must be "organized and licensed under State law as a risk-bearing entity eligible to offer health insurance or health benefits coverage in each State in which it offers a Medicare+Choice plan" [Social Security Act, §1855(a)]. However, as discussed more fully below, the secretary may waive the licensing requirement under certain conditions.
15. Social Security Act, §1855(d); 42 CFR 422.350(b).
16. To meet the "substantial financial risk" test, *each* affiliated provider shall be required to share in the risk of operating the Medicare PSO. 42 CFR § 422.356(a).
17. In determining whether an IPA, for instance, qualifies as an "affiliated provider," an IPA would need to demonstrate that it is engaged in the delivery of services (or, more likely, is organized and operated primarily for the purpose of providing such services) and that the members control the IPA.
18. In this context, control is presumed to exist if one party directly or indirectly owns, controls, or holds the power to vote or proxies for 51 percent of the voting rights or governance rights of another. 42 CFR § 422.354(d).
19. The waiver process terminates in 2002, but waivers issued prior to that date will last the full three years.
20. Waiver request forms are presently available via the HCFA Internet site.
21. 42 CFR § 422.372.
22. Social Security Act, §1852(e). Moreover, the BBA calls for a QA program in each plan, periodic surveys of members to assess their satisfaction with the plan, and dissemination of information on plan performance during the open enrollment process.

23. Social Security Act, §1852(b).
24. Social Security Act, §1853.
25. For 1998, the minimum payment is $367 per member per month.
26. As a result of these provisions and their interaction, approximately 60 percent of counties received a 2 percent increase from their 1997 AAPPC rate, with the remaining counties receiving the minimum payment of $367.
27. The Balanced Budget Act requires the secretary to establish procedures for enrollment and disenrollment in Medicare+Choice options. Newly eligible enrollees who do not choose a Medicare+Choice plan are deemed to have chosen the original Medicare fee-for-service arrangement, with certain limited exceptions. Social Security Act, §1851(c).
28. Social Security Act, §1851.
29. See "Medicare Comparer" on the HCFA Internet site.
30. Interestingly, the secretary may enter into contracts with nonfederal entities to carry out the information dissemination activities. The secretary has required plans to pay their pro rata share of the cost of information dissemination.
31. Social Security Act, §1851(h).
32. Social Security Act, §1856.
33. A March 5, 1998, committee statement sets forth numerous PSO solvency recommendations with which the members concur.
34. The committee was comprised of 15 individuals representing physicians and physician groups, hospitals, insurers, rural providers, long-term care providers, beneficiaries, state insurance commissioners, and the administration. Individual members of the committee were selected by the interests they represented.
35. 42 CFR § 422.380 through 422.390.
36. 42 CFR § 422.382. The regulations give HCFA the discretion to lower this standard to $1 million based on a business/financial plan demonstrating that the PSO has or has available to it an administrative infrastructure that will reduce the PSO's start-up costs.
37. Other intangible assets include physician contracts, practice management agreements, and health care delivery networks.
38. Thus, HCFA will admit the GAAP value of intangible assets up to 20 percent of the minimum net worth required if at least the greater of $1 million or 67 percent of the ongoing minimum net worth is met by cash or cash equivalents. If this is not the case, HCFA will admit the GAAP value of intangible assets up to 10 percent. 42 CFR § 422.382.

39. 42 CFR § 422.384(d). Guarantees will be acceptable as a resource to meet projected losses under certain specified conditions. Moreover, an irrevocable, unconditional letter of credit may be used in place of cash or cash equivalents if satisfactory to HCFA.
40. It is anticipated that the regulations will contain the same hold harmless and continuation of coverage/benefit rules for PSOs as for other Medicare Part C contractors. Accordingly, it is likely that PSOs would remain responsible for coverage during the period of payment and after the period of payment until hospital discharge occurs.

Chapter 3

Critical Success Factors for Provider Sponsored Organizations

Bruce Gosser

Provider sponsored organizations (PSOs) present tremendous opportunities for innovative groups of providers with a command of a wide range of health care services and a healthy respect for the disciplines of risk assumption. As provider fee-for-service reimbursement levels are capped, the opportunity to assume risk and achieve higher profitability by eliminating inefficient and unnecessary services will help offset the impact of flattened reimbursement in the regular Medicare program.

However, insurance risk is a complex and difficult area, and many provider groups have found managing reductions in health care costs to be far more difficult than creating additional programs and services for the elderly and thereby boosting provider revenues (and, consequently, boosting health care costs). Since the PSO provides a new way to deal with Medicare risk, few exact models exist. However, the successful and failed managed care initiatives, especially provider-led initiatives, in the past several years offer important guidance. Here are a few of the elements that will likely contribute to success:

- market knowledge and a market focus
- an effective sales and marketing plan
- adequate capitalization
- physician leadership and commitment

- a shared vision
- the alignment of incentives and medical cost predictability
- information system capacity to monitor cost and utilization
- a comprehensive provider network
- an efficient infrastructure
- competitive and unique benefit plans
- a wide range of management expertise

MARKET KNOWLEDGE AND A MARKET FOCUS

Community providers have an edge when it comes to knowledge of the local market. Hospitals and hospital systems are particularly advantaged in this regard, as many possess substantial pertinent data and a deep understanding of their markets. However, a hospital's knowledge of its market usually is focused on the delivery side, not on the health plan, insurer, or payer side. Knowing the managed care plan competitors and the prospective competitors will be critical to PSO success. Exhibit 3–1 suggests a methodology for analyzing the health plan and payer segment of the Medicare market.

An analysis of the market, including the characteristics of health plan and PSO competitors, can shape the strategy of the emerging PSO. Designing a PSO around careful analysis of what is available (or planned) in the market will help to ensure that the program is market focused. Benefit plan design is viewed as an important competitive factor among seniors and commercial populations, but it is often unfamiliar to providers. For this reason, benefit plan design has been highlighted in this chapter.

The market analysis must also include a careful analysis of the demographic characteristics of the senior population. Where do the seniors live? What are their interests, values, needs, and goals? How ready to accept change are they? This will be a critical question. Almost 25 years after the Health Maintenance Organization (HMO) Act of 1973, many states have less than 10 percent total HMO enrollment, and most of this enrollment is in commercial, non-Medicare sectors. Medicare seniors generally

Exhibit 3–1 Medicare Market Analysis Factors

Structure and background
Years of managed care experience
Years of Medicare risk experience
Medicare enrollment trend
Ownership and governance

Sales and marketing
Direct sales force or broker strategy
Media advertising approach and budget
Market segments targeted
Benefit plan designs offered
Incentives offered to enrollees

Financial performance
Historic financial performance
Medical loss ratio
Profitability
General and administrative expenses
Pricing aggressiveness (overall)
Capital reserves

Provider network
Comprehensiveness of network
Geographic coverage
Gatekeeper/open access panels
Ratio of and access to primary care
Provider rate structure and discounts
Exclusivity in provider contracting

constitute the most conservative population segment, so the PSO will face a serious challenge in trying to stimulate change in this segment.

A unique advantage possessed by provider sponsored initiatives is the close, trusting relationship with seniors that many providers enjoy. A Florida consumer survey among seniors revealed that 80 percent rated physician and hospital ownership "very important." Over 90 percent also considered as very important the fact that a plan was locally owned and governed.

Providers that have studied the demographics of the elderly can put their data and knowledge to good use. In fact, some traditional insurers object to the PSO concept because local providers often have an advantage in marketing products to seniors and are well placed to market only to the healthier sectors of the senior populations.

AN EFFECTIVE SALES AND MARKETING PLAN

Turning market knowledge into a dynamic and effective sales and marketing plan is the next challenge in developing a PSO. Health care organizations have little background in developing and managing a sales force. They have usually restricted themselves to advertising, public relations activities, and networking (particularly with physician customers). On the other hand, from the very beginning managed care plans and their precursors, health insurance companies, have risen or fallen on the strength of sales effectiveness. Note, however, that sales strategy in the Medicare risk arena is vastly different from sales strategy in the commercial health insurance market. Group health insurance sold commercially is distributed to employers, often through insurance brokers. Traditional health insurance companies are often confused and frustrated by the one-on-one sales approach required by the senior market.

As mentioned above, the affiliation between providers and seniors can be a tremendous advantage. Enhancing the trust that already exists through promotional materials and public relations events and activities and making use of the trust in the detailed research phase of sales plan development will be vital to PSO success. Many hospitals offer social club–type senior care programs to community residents and former patients. The organized activities characteristic of these programs can create a wealth of goodwill and at the same time function as a source for lead generation.

An emerging PSO will survive and gain strength in the market through early attraction of a nucleus of members and steady growth in enrollment thereafter. To achieve these objectives, careful planning will be essential. The planning should allow for bold midcourse corrections if the initial strategies fail to generate an adequate response. Sales success, while important in any business, is especially critical for PSOs for two important reasons: PSO development will be costly and time consuming if done properly and thoroughly, and PSO infrastructure represents a fixed overhead cost, which will be a drain on capital until the plan reaches the break-even point.

Another fact to keep in mind is that the PSO's amassed capital will be important in future years as a reserve to protect against the fluctuation in claims. The problem is that the outflow of funds to reach break-even could deplete the capital reserves necessary for the financial strength of the plan in the long term. An early demonstration PSO project in Ohio was operational after six months of careful planning and development, within the targeted time frame. Such a time frame should be considered appropriately aggressive for most markets. Whether it can be achieved will depend on the existing level of managed care expertise and the organized structures available from the beginning.

The physician partnerships so essential to PSO survival demand early sales success as well. Financial investments are highly personal for most physicians, probably because they balance the use of funds for investment against their use for lifestyle enhancements. For this reason, physicians will be excited by and committed to the project if they begin seeing PSO patients in their practice (return on investment) almost immediately. In other words, physician support and goodwill, important success factors, can be bolstered through high levels of early enrollment.

ADEQUATE CAPITALIZATION

A comprehensive business plan will guide the determination of the appropriate capitalization levels. How much is enough? That question can only be answered after a careful evaluation of the market opportunity, the number and approach of competitors, the level of risk to be assumed by the PSO, and the infrastructure components needed in order for the organization to effectively compete in the market.

It is imperative to include an actuarial projection of the capital required for insuring risk and meeting statutory reserve requirements. Provider managed care venture failures, such as the recent closure of a physician-hospital contracting network with 33,000 members in one midwestern community, should alert providers to the importance of adequate capitalization. The overwhelming reason for such failures has been a lack of capital and a failure to understand and plan for the sizable amount of capital required by state statutes and regulatory entities.

Like any other business, PSOs must have capital to build up business and cover costs through break-even. As regulated risk bearing entities, however, PSOs will be required to have reserved capital on its balance sheet to protect against fluctuating income and expenditures. State commercial guidelines and the industry guidelines established by the National Association of Insurance Commissioners (NAIC) will be helpful in sizing the level of capital needed for insurance reserves. A general rule is that there should be a three-to-one ratio of premiums to reserves. Therefore, for every $3 million in premium, a PSO may need a balance sheet surplus of $1 million.

Table 3–1 illustrates the relationship between enrollment growth, premium revenue, and reserve requirements in a traditional managed care company. The numbers are not presented to frighten provider organizations or deter them from entering the PSO marketplace. Reserve requirements can be minimized through reinsurance relationships and provider risk contracts. The alignment of provider risk and provider incentives is a critical success factor discussed later in this chapter.

PHYSICIAN LEADERSHIP AND COMMITMENT

Physician leadership and the commitment of all physician participants will be crucial to PSO success. Hospitals and hospital systems will be the first to study and develop PSO initiatives,

Table 3–1 Sample Enrollments, Premiums, and Surplus Requirements

Enrollment	*Monthly Premium*	*Annual Premium*	*Surplus Required*
1,000	$380	$ 4,560,000	$ 1,520,000
5,000	380	22,800,000	7,600,000
20,000	380	91,200,000	30,000,000

Note: Based on estimates from NAIC guidelines.

because of their capital resources, strategic planning perspective, and easy access to outside expertise. Physicians and hospitals will necessarily become partners in the PSO framework, owing to the requirement that the ownership of a PSO encompass a substantial proportion of all health care services.

Physicians order most health care services and procedures. Further, physicians are the most highly trained professionals in the health care delivery system and are best able to develop cost-effective treatment guidelines. Committed physicians will accept substantial risk and manage this risk more effectively. The commitment of physicians will result in more satisfied members, members who sense that their physicians support them in their choice of health plan option.

Physician commitment should not be assumed, nor treated lightly. Physicians must be involved early and completely in the planning stages of the initiative. They must see and react to the financial projections, including the investment requirements, expected flow of health care expenditures, and projections of profitability or loss. Any risks associated with premature disclosure of the development plans will be offset by the benefits achieved by establishing a core group of committed physician leaders who will spread the message among their colleagues.

Hospitals and health systems may confront fallout resulting from earlier attempts at integration. The Humana decision to divest itself of its hospitals many years ago is perhaps the most obvious example of a clash between the interests of a hospital or system and physicians with regard to a managed care initiative. Up to 30 percent of hospitals in highly competitive markets report the presence of a physician hospital organization (PHO), and 32 percent report the presence of a physician-sponsored individual practice association (IPA). About 18–20 percent of hospitals employ physicians in medium to highly competitive managed care markets.[1] Throughout the industry, however, hospital and system PHO development and practice acquisition strategies have emphasized the differences between hospitals and physicians. At the same time, many physicians, particularly in primary care specialties, have learned to coexist with managed care plans quite effectively. Managed care plans entering the Medicare risk field as competitors of a PSO already bring commercial patients to the physicians and may be sharing risk with the physicians with respect to that business segment. Each of these factors represent a challenge in integrating successfully with physicians in the PSO framework.

A SHARED VISION

The Medicare+Choice legislation requires a substantial proportion of the health care services under a PSO Medicare contract be provided directly through the provider or group of affiliated providers. The provider or affiliated providers must share substantial financial risk, either directly or indirectly, and have a majority financial interest. The regulations clearly intend for providers across various components of the industry to bear substantial risk and have ownership.

Although sponsored by providers, risk-bearing PSOs take on many of the characteristics of payers. As provider PSO leaders think and react like payers, a clash of priorities can be predicted. In developing or sponsoring a PSO, the initial motivation of many providers is to protect the Medicare market and forestall insurance company encroachment into the Medicare arena. Provider backlash against managed care tactics and procedures will inspire PSO development in some communities and among some provider groups.

What is the primary reason to develop a PSO in your community? The following questions suggest some of the issues that typically confront providers tempted to embark on a PSO initiative:

- Is the goal to return more dollars to the providers or increase the cost-effectiveness of health care delivery overall?
- Is the PSO expected to maximize revenue at the plan level or at the provider level?
- Is the PSO expected to lessen pressure on provider utilization practices or to tighten these patterns and outcomes?
- Will providers be educated about utilization infractions or be censured or both?
- Is the PSO designed to grow the membership to the highest levels or to balance growth with stable risk?
- Will providers bear the risk and profit potential evenly or will the risks or rewards be shifted to one side or the other?
- Will the initial capital primarily come from the hospital, the physicians, or another source?
- Where will additional capital be generated as needed, and how will control be impacted by additional capital contributions?

These issues confront providers at the inception of PSO development and again at various critical junctures. HealthLink, a 560,000 member commercial managed care plan in St. Louis, was sold to Blue Cross and Blue Shield of Missouri in 1995 primarily because of the conflict in vision among its provider owners (nine major metropolitan hospitals and an insurer). For that plan, the conflicts developed and deepened some 10 years after the plan had developed.

THE ALIGNMENT OF INCENTIVES AND MEDICAL COST PREDICTABILITY

One strategy to contain the amount of capital required is to structure the provider reimbursement in such a way as to fix the variation in health care cost expenditures. Health care costs can be made predictable through a number of provider reimbursement strategies, including capitation of primary care, specialists, hospitals, and all other segments of the industry. Global budgeting, a variation on capitation, combines fee for service with fixed expenditures. Capitation can be determined by fixed rates or by percentage of premium. In the commercial managed care arena, Mutual of Omaha was an early leader in developing percentage-of-premium contracts with providers (it initiated such contracts almost ten years ago). Each of these strategies can relieve some of the surplus reserve requirements for a PSO if regulators are convinced that risk variability is borne by providers directly and not by the PSO entity.

Another strategy for sharing risk is to place provider withholds in a risk pool, with gains and losses shared among the providers. A performance incentive system can offer providers a share of savings below targeted costs without requiring participation in risk from medical losses. Potential provider gains from such systems are usually minimal, since the providers are not sharing in downside losses. Many experts cite the importance of risk sharing in Medicare risk: "In many ways the risk model is the key to success because it provides the reinforcement of the managed care principles needed to successfully manage a risk contract."[2]

Fixed cost reimbursement can be valuable in aligning provider incentives and contributing to a common vision for the PSO partners. When all or most providers share risk, they quickly determine where to land on the questions of profitability to the plan, provider unit rates, the role of utilization management, the importance of sanctions for inefficient providers, and so on.

Capitation or a related strategy will only be effective when applied fairly and uniformly and communicated clearly to providers in advance of contracting. PSO leaders and developers should not assume that the participating providers possess a high level of understanding of the details or dynamics of capitation reimbursement. Capitation is relatively new to providers in most areas of the country. Medicare risk involves different actuarial profiles and delivery system dynamics than commercial risk populations and budgets do.

INFORMATION SYSTEM CAPACITY TO MONITOR COST AND UTILIZATION

Providers have been calling for clear, accurate, and timely reporting of health cost data for years. Health care delivery and financing are responsible for an overwhelming volume of highly intricate, detailed data points. The average commercially covered person generates four to five health insurance claims per year. The average covered senior in a Medicare risk program generates 15 to 20 health claims per year, making the provision of accurate and timely data in understandable formats an heroic achievement. Meeting participating provider expectations in this area will help to ensure that an informed and committed network of providers exists. Sitting down with provider representatives to determine what management reports are needed and to design them before the inception of the PSO will help to make expectations more reasonable and thus offer a better opportunity for success.

Providers approach data far differently than insurance executives and many actuaries. Providers are interested in frequency of procedures and primary care, specialty physician, outpatient, hospital inpatient, pharmacy, and out-of-area expenditures. A presentation of appropriate cost and frequency data in the aggregate and on a per member per month (pmpm) basis can be very useful to a provider group in determining problem areas and potential solutions. The ability to generate detailed reports to specific provider and specific member experiences also will be important.

A paradox exists for PSOs intent on provider capitation reimbursement and improving information reporting. Typically, the most reliable data in the insurance industry at present are claims data. Providers rely more heavily on utilization data, which is more costly to retrieve and more subjective. Provider capitation has been shown to result in submission of incomplete claims and encounter data to the plan because of the lessened incentive for the provider, who has already been paid for the services (through the prepayment of capitation). PSO physician and hospital leaders need to embrace this paradox in designing the program to balance expected results.

A COMPREHENSIVE PROVIDER NETWORK

A comprehensive provider network is highly marketable to seniors. The PSO legislation calls for broad-based provider participation in health care delivery, in risk sharing, and even in PSO ownership. The health care delivery system today is highly fragmented, and the intent of the Medicare+Choice legislation appears to be to generate needed consolidation. Figure 3–1 shows the many segments of the health care industry arranged in a structure, from managed care to primary care physicians.

Seniors will select the managed care option that offers the widest choice of physicians and hospitals. Throughout the United States, seniors report stronger physician loyalty than any other segment of the population. Established relationships with providers appear to be less important to seniors only in parts of

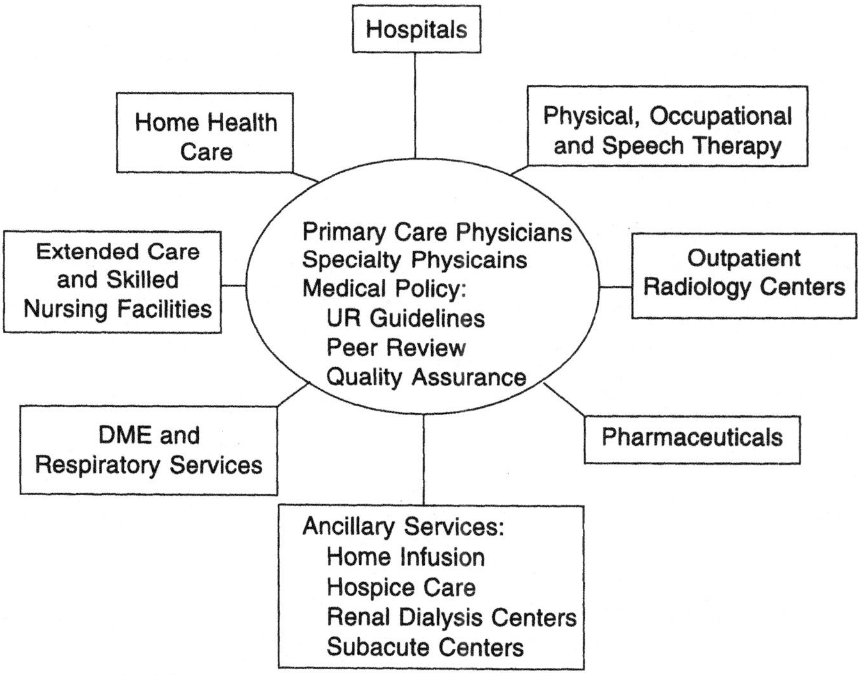

Figure 3–1 An approach to organizing the delivery of health care. Courtesy of Heartland Health, Inc., Topeka, Kansas.

the Sunbelt, like Florida, Arizona, and southern California, where seniors have relocated for retirement.

The strong affiliation between seniors and their providers presents interesting opportunities and challenges for PSO participants. The opportunities have already been discussed. The challenges derive from the fact that many of the "preferred providers" of the targeted senior population will not be in the PSO. In many instances, those providers were omitted for a reason, such as questions regarding the quality of their care provision or a desire on the part of the founders of the PSO to create a narrow network market opportunity for themselves. The result is that crucial questions will quickly arise:

- Will the PSO invite competitors into the network?
- Will the PSO expand to accept marginally qualified providers because of consumer preference?
- Will competing managed care plans include those providers in networks for seniors? If so, how will the PSO persuade seniors to choose it as their health care plan?

These issues are complex and often difficult to resolve in a provider-sponsored managed care plan. Providers frequently decide health plan issues from their perspective as providers, not as the owners of a managed care entity. The two perspectives can clash when matters of exclusivity and competition at the provider level come into play. Given the broad-based support and ownership intended in the Medicare+Choice legislation, those issues could severely challenge the structure, vision, and commitment of its provider owners from the beginning.

AN EFFICIENT INFRASTRUCTURE

The successful PSO will find creative ways to minimize the development of the costly insurance infrastructure needed to support traditional managed care plans. Figure 3–2 shows the various functional areas and interrelationships within a regulated managed care plan.

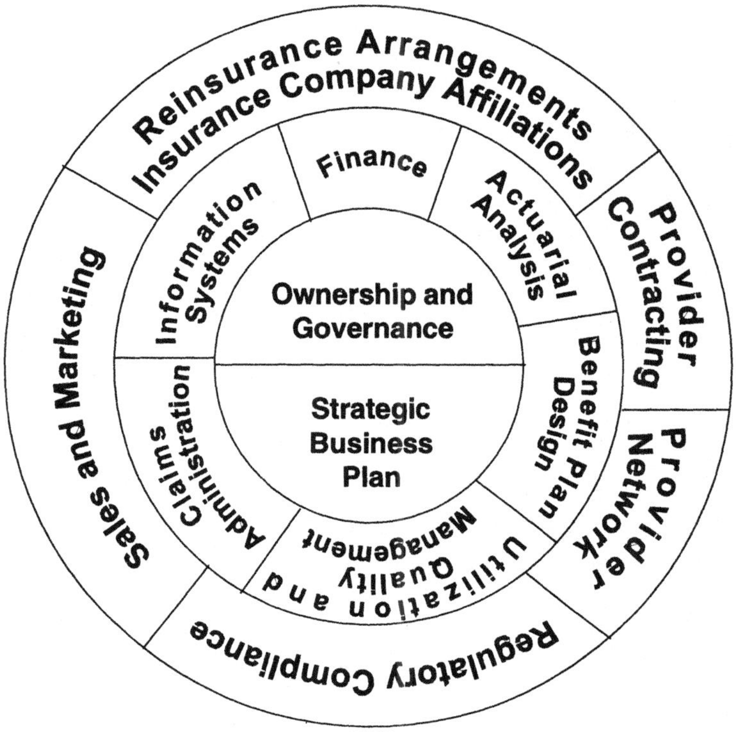

Figure 3–2 Functions and relationships of a managed care organization.

The PSO will be challenged to find ways of covering all the critical areas involved in managing care while minimizing the build up of duplicative and costly infrastructure. Managed care infrastructure in commercial plans ranges from about 9 percent of total premiums to as high as 25 percent (for some established plans with lower enrollment). Medicare risk premiums are typically three times the level of commercial premiums, and the administrative cost should be kept at the lower end of this range for total services. Utilization management and information systems are critical areas of infrastructure that should not be short-changed in the process of holding down administrative costs, however. The high costs of medical services warrant highly effective measures of monitoring and controlling these costs.

One way to minimize infrastructure costs is to outsource or to partner with managed care plans, possibly in the commercial market, to acquire needed infrastructure. If an existing plan has excess capacity and is able to offer services at an incremental cost, outsourcing or partnering could be very beneficial in the areas of information systems, claims administration, utilization management, and possibly network management. Numerous opportunities for partnering should be available, given the pressure on managed care plans to reduce infrastructure costs (best done through gaining volume) and the interest of many plans to enter the Medicare market in some form. Partnering may be more effective than a straight outsourcing relationship, at least if the partnership includes risk sharing, sharing quality and efficiency standards, and other mechanisms for the commercial partner to participate in the PSO. Sharing will make many vendors of managed care infrastructure more committed and more responsive to improvement in service.

Minimizing infrastructure also can be achieved through various risk arrangements with providers. Global capitation of providers should reduce the cost of both claims administration and utilization management at the plan level while delegating the responsibility and authority for these functions to the provider along with the risk. This approach can be problematic if planwide data are not available or are separated into many different databases. In holding down administrative costs, each plan must strike its own balance.

COMPETITIVE BENEFIT PLANS

All Medicare+Choice plans must cover basic mandated Medicare benefits, but each may also offer additional basic and supplemental benefits. PSOs and other Medicare plans may require cost sharing from enrollees through deductibles, copayments, or coinsurance and may even charge additional premiums. Enrollee cost sharing may not exceed cost sharing in the traditional Medicare program. If additional premiums are charged, rebates will be denied as a form of incentive to enroll or to remain in a specific plan. PSO designers will want to study the level of benefits offered by existing plans to determine the best strategies for the specific market.

In developing competitive benefit plans for the senior market in a particular service area, providers should consider demographic characteristics of the local market as well as actuarial trends for the market population. Demographic and actuarial analysis could aid in the development of benefit plans designed to correct adverse utilization trends (e.g., lack of affiliation with primary care physicians, overuse of hospital emergency departments, and over- or underutilization of pharmacy benefits). Health care service utilization can be significantly altered through the adjustment of benefits, particularly through the institution of copays and deductibles.

PSO benefit designers should consider the changing patterns and practices in regular Medicare stimulated by the Medicare+Choice legislation. Significant additional coverage has been added to regular Medicare for wellness and prevention services. Deductibles are being waived for screening mammograms for women over age 40. Similarly, screening pelvic exams and Pap smears will no longer be subject to deductibles. Additional coverage is being included for prostate cancer screening, colorectal screening, influenza vaccination, pneumococcal vaccination, diabetes screening, and bone mass measurement for certain individuals. The changes in the regular Medicare program will have significant ramifications for the PSO seeking to differentiate itself from competitors and its coverage from the status quo coverage for seniors.

Even in an arena like Medicare risk, where plan design options are limited, substantial time and professional benefits expertise should be applied to ensure that the benefit offerings of the PSO are market based and appropriately constructed. Benefit plan design is both a sales and marketing tool and an important means of encouraging enrolled members to utilize services when they should be utilized. The necessary skills and background are foreign to most health care providers, and providers should turn to knowledgeable consultants, health actuaries, benefits consultants, and health care underwriters for expertise.

Ideally the consultants will have previous experience in Medicare risk as part of their background.

Market-based benefit plans make the PSO more attractive to consumers and aid in achieving the early sales success that is so important to covering overhead, minimizing start-up costs, and bringing patients to the physician offices. When the plan designs also motivate enrollees to access primary care physicians appropriately and to order prescriptions in a cost-effective manner, they are helping essential utilization patterns to begin to form.

A WIDE RANGE OF MANAGEMENT EXPERTISE

In many markets across the United States, the proliferation of managed care initiatives among providers has resulted in a serious shortage of experienced professionals with the background and expertise needed to lead PSO development efforts. Because of its structure, a PSO requires expertise in a wide range of functional areas, including sales and marketing, benefit plan design development, actuarial analysis, financial management, regulatory compliance, utilization management, quality management, and information systems. In short, successful development requires an executive leadership skilled at bringing together trained staff and experienced consultants to work collectively on a large, complex project. The trend toward consolidation in more developed managed care markets has resulted in the availability of some individuals with managed care talent, but providers have found that not all of these individuals are completely in tune with the vision and complexities of provider-sponsored managed care initiatives.

In staffing for PSO development, these guidelines should be followed:

- Seek a senior executive with the right vision and a demonstrated ability to work with provider groups and handle highly complex, multifaceted projects.

- Locate experienced consultants in specialized areas (e.g., actuarial analysis, benefits design, and information systems).
- Outsource key functions if the right fit can be attained. In an outsourcing arrangement, seek experienced, successful partners with excess capacity, aligned incentives, and a willingness to share control and communicate openly.
- Place experienced staff in key areas, like sales, utilization management, and claims administration.
- For lower, functional positions, hire capable staff with high energy, a strong motivation, and the ability to learn quickly.
- Set out clear, measurable goals for staff and consultants and communicate frequently about milestones and barriers to achieving those goals.

CONCLUSION

Success in developing a PSO will depend on a wide range of critical factors. Providers contemplating PSO development should not be deterred because of the task's complexity. They may confront a far greater challenge maintaining current clinical revenues and profits in the face of changes in the regular Medicare program, such as caps on reimbursement and the stimulation of competition among managed care plans.

The Balanced Budget Act of 1997 contains reductions in disproportionate share payments to hospitals through 2002, combined with reduced prospective payment system (PPS) capital payment rates for all hospitals and reduced reimbursement for indirect medical education. The act contains significant reimbursement caps and changes in Part B for physician services as well.

Unaffiliated providers in smaller markets may find it necessary to affiliate with initiatives structured by larger, more integrated health care delivery systems. Another strategy may be to link with Medicare HMOs in collaborative, risk-sharing ventures. Affiliation with a managed care plan, assuming the risk arrangement is well designed and fair, can offer providers many benefits.

Advocate Health Care Network, an integrated health care delivery network in Chicago, is working to craft a Medicare risk arrangement with Humana, the publicly traded HMO, for the Chicago market.[3] Generally, provider groups with established expertise in managed care will have a distinct advantage, even if the managed care programs have been limited to commercial lines. Provider groups with managed care plan ownership in HMOs, preferred provider organizations, or risk-bearing management service organizations or independent practice associations will find the experience they have gained to be a good foundation—and might find the ownership itself to provide an organizational and economic base—for PSO development.

Although dealing with Medicare risk through a PSO will be an experiment for most providers, the market response from providers and traditional managed care plans is expected to accelerate. Thus, Medicare will become competitive at the plan level to a much greater degree than previously. Providers are advised to participate in PSOs at some level of ownership and risk assumption. Otherwise, increasing control over medical care will revert to insurance-based operations. Perhaps a caution often applied to the stock market is appropriate: Do not risk more (in the beginning, at least) than you can reasonably afford to lose.

NOTES

1. "Putting Managed Care in Its Place," *Hospitals and Health Networks*, 5 January, 1998.
2. H.A. Levin, P.A. Zenner, R.A. Kipp, and E.L. Whitney, "Provider-based Medicare Risk Contracting and Subcontracting: Opportunities and Risks for Provider Sponsored Organizations," *Managed Care Quarterly* 5, no. 4 (1997): 18–33.
3. *Provider Sponsored Managed Care Companies: The Search for the New Paradigm* (New York: Shattuck Hammond, Partners, 1997).

CHAPTER 4

Key Legal Issues for Provider Sponsored Organizations

Wendy L. Krasner and Patrick K. O'Hare

This chapter reviews key legal issues raised by the establishment of a provider sponsored organization (PSO), including the contracts it needs to enter into for qualification as a PSO, and the operation of the entity as a Medicare+Choice contractor.[1]

The Health Care Financing Administration (HCFA) has recently published interim final rules to define PSOs (63 *Fed. Reg.* 18124-18135, April 14, 1998) and to establish PSO waiver and solvency requirements (63 *Fed. Reg.* 25360-25379, May 7, 1998). However, at the current time, HCFA has not yet issued the interim final Part C rules that will establish the requirements for Medicare+Choice contractors. The Balanced Budget Act of 1997 (BBA) had required that these rules be published by June 1, 1998. Thus, in the absence of specific Medicare+Choice rules, the analysis herein relies in many instances on the statutory provisions in the BBA. It is important to note that, while these new Part C rules will build on the current Medicare risk contract framework contained at 42 CFR § 417.400 et seq., it is expected that the rules may contain significant new regulatory requirements. Third, sometime in the early fall of 1998, HCFA will make available the actual new Medicare+Choice contracts that all plans, including PSOs, will be required to enter into in order to participate in the new program. It is not yet known how different the contract will be from the current Medicare risk agreement, nor whether the contract will contain provisions that apply uniquely to PSOs.[2] Thus, there are several key legal terms applicable to PSOs that are not available at the time of this writing. Because much of what we know at this point comes from the BBA, many of the references in the chapter are to this act. Indeed, all section citations, unless otherwise noted, are to the act or to its legislative history (Public Law 105-33, III Stat. 251 [August 5, 1997]; H.R. Conf. Rep. no. 105-217).

It needs to be noted that there are really two types of PSOs. The first type needs a federal waiver from state risk-bearing entity licensure requirements. For ease of reference, this type will be referred to as a federally waived PSO (FW-PSO). The other type is a PSO that has obtained state licensure as a risk-bearing entity but also seeks the PSO designation to take advantage of certain other, albeit limited, PSO benefits (described below). HCFA clearly takes the position that such a state-licensed entity may qualify as a PSO if it meets the definition. This type of PSO will be referred to as a state-licensed PSO. The term "PSO" is used to mean both FW-PSOs and state-licensed PSOs.

PSO FORMATION

Critical to structuring a successful PSO will be selection of a corporate structure that not only facilitates the PSO's business objective but also satisfies HCFA's requirements for PSO structure and contracting. Salient structuring and contracting issues are discussed below.

As noted above, HCFA recently promulgated regulations that further define the eligibility requirements for PSOs. An entity wishing to consider PSO development must look to the statute and to these regulations for guidance as to how to structure its PSO. The regulations include both key definitional terms and solvency standards (which as described elsewhere in this chapter, are relevant for PSOs seeking a HCFA waiver from state licensing requirements).

The Statutory Definition

Section 1855(d) of the Medicare Act (as added by section 4001 of the BBA) defines PSOs as

> a public or private entity—
>
> (A) that is established or organized, and operated, by a health care provider, or group of affiliated health care providers,
>
> (B) that provides a substantial proportion[3] . . . of the health care items and services under the contract . . . through the provider or [an] affiliated group of providers, and
>
> (C) with respect to which the affiliated providers share, directly or indirectly, substantial financial risk with respect to the provision of such items and services and have at least a majority financial interest in the entity. (Footnote added.)

Simply put, for purposes of meeting the statutory definition of a PSO, the PSO applicant must be either a single provider (e.g., a single integrated delivery system [IDS] or academic medical center with a significant number of employed physicians) or a group of "affiliated" providers. HCFA has defined "health care provider" to include an individual or entity licensed by the state and "engaged in the delivery of health care services."[4] In the case of an entity (rather than an individual) the latter term means that the entity is "organized and operated primarily for the purpose" of providing health care directly or through its provider members.[5] Providers are affiliated under section 1855(d)(3)

> if through contract, ownership, or otherwise—
>
> (A) one provider, directly or indirectly, controls, is controlled by, or is under common control with the other,
>
> (B) both providers are part of a controlled group of corporations under section 1563 of the Internal Revenue Code,[6]
>
> (C) each provider is a participant in a lawful combination under which each provider shares substantial fi-

> nancial risk in connection with the organization's operations, or
>
> (D) both providers are part of an affiliated service group under section 414 of such Code.[7] (Footnotes added.)

For purposes of satisfying this definition of affiliation, most PSO applicants will utilize the test of subparagraph C (the sharing of "substantial financial risk"), as the other three tests typically will not apply.

Applicants for PSO status will need to meet the "affiliated" test of subsection (d)(1) (which requires that the "affiliated providers" share directly or indirectly substantial financial risk *and* have a majority financial interest in the entity) as well as the "affiliated" test of subsection (d)(3)(C) (which requires each provider to share "substantial financial risk" in connection with the organization's operations). HCFA has elaborated on the second prong of the first test of "affiliated" in its PSO definitional regulations. In essence, providers can satisfy this part of the test if they maintain effective control over the PSO.[8] Significantly, this test does not need to be satisfied by *all* of the affiliated providers; it is sufficient if the requisite control is exercised by just a small subset of the providers (which HCFA explains could be as few as just a single provider).[9] These tests suggest several planning points discussed below.

First, HCFA has defined "substantial financial risk" for purposes of subsection (d)(1) and subsection (d)(3) in a similar fashion, borrowing heavily from antitrust concepts. Hallmarks of the sharing of substantial financial risk include percentage of premium arrangements, global capitation, and fee-for-service with substantial withholding arrangements. The key to satisfying the antitrust definition is for the providers to share horizontal risk (i.e., provider A suffers the consequences of the utilization decisions of provider B and vice versa). Arrangements where each provider is individually capitated and is at risk only for his or her own delivery of services within an individual financial budget are not sufficient.

Second, the requirement to share substantial financial risk suggests that PSO applicants should consider the creation of a *new* entity to serve as the PSO. Many existing managed care contracting organizations (including physician-hospital organizations [PHOs] and management service organizations [MSOs]) have a substantial amount of fee-for-service, nonrisk business, and it is possible that HCFA would conclude that these providers do not share sufficient risk to meet the definition. By contrast, a new entity established only for the PSO line of business would be able to meet the test, assuming its Medicare Part C services were the only services it offered.

Third, creation of a new entity raises the question of how the applicant will satisfy the minimum PSO enrollment requirements (1,500 members for urban areas and 500 members for rural areas). Perhaps the best solution to this "Catch 22" problem is for the applicant to seek a waiver of the minimum threshold requirements from HCFA. Waivers are permitted during a three-year start-up period.[10]

Fourth, care should be exercised when using an independent practice association (IPA) or physician practice management (PPM) company as the appropriate corporate entity to seek PSO qualification. Because many of these entities are organized and operated to either arrange for the delivery of care (in the case of an IPA) or to manage providers' practices (in the case of a PPM), both may not satisfy the definition of "health care provider" which, as noted above, requires that the entity be organized and operated to directly provide care.

Finally, despite the requirement in subsection (d)(1) that the PSO entity be "established or organized, and operated" by a provider or a group of affiliated providers, it will be permissible for PSOs to purchase management services. Consistent with HCFA's desire to define the PSO criteria in such a way as to include as many qualified applicants as possible, HCFA has indicated in various meetings that PSOs will be allowed to purchase needed management services and will not have to provide the entire PSO management infrastructure itself.

Governance Implications

These risk-sharing requirements have obvious implications for PSO structuring. Although the regulations would allow governance to be centralized in but a few providers, the need to share in the governance widely if not directly imposed by HCFA, likely will be a political reality. Thus, providers whose contracts put them at risk for the financial success or failure of the PSO will most likely want some share in the governance of the organization, by providing, for example, input on essential business issues, such as how the Medicare adjusted average per capita cost (AAPCC) payment will be divided by the affiliated providers, the composition of risk pools, utilization and quality assurance procedures, provider grievances, and the terms of provider agreements. The PSO's ultimate structure will need to accommodate the sharing of governance among the participating providers.

The Solvency Requirements

In addition to the statutory definitions set forth above, providers considering how best to structure PSOs will also need to take account of the solvency requirements applicable to PSOs seeking federal waivers of state licensing requirements. Although a complete discussion of the solvency requirements appears elsewhere in this text (see "Fiscal Solvency: Put Up or Shut Up?" in Chapter 2), they are summarized here for ready reference.

At the initial application stage, a PSO applicant will need a minimum net worth of $1.5 million. HCFA can reduce this in appropriate cases to $1 million. At least $750,000 must be in cash. The applicant must submit an explanation of how it plans to cover projected operating losses; a guarantee from a hospital (or other providers with sufficient assets) can be used to cover the losses, assuming the guarantee meets various timing and other requirements. Significantly, health care delivery system assets (e.g., hospital buildings) can be counted toward satisfying these requirements *only* if the assets are appropriately represented on the balance sheet of the PSO, not on the balance sheet of the hospital owner of the assets.

For the ongoing phase of the PSO, HCFA has proposed multiple net worth tests based on various minimum fixed cash requirements or percentages of premium and expenses. Again, a liquidity requirement is imposed to ensure that the entity will have sufficient cash available to pay claims and other expenses.[11]

Tax Implications for PSO Structuring

As is evident from the stringent solvency requirements (which essentially focus on liquid assets and will not realistically allow most PSOs to count the delivery system assets of their affiliated hospital providers), it will be necessary for the affiliated providers to contribute cash to the federally-waivered PSO sufficient to meet HCFA's solvency requirements. Although it might appear most convenient to have the hospital (or hospitals) participating in the PSO simply contribute this money, any participating tax-exempt hospital, in the event that it contributed capital in amounts disproportionate to its share of the organization's governance, would face a significant tax risk.

The Internal Revenue Service (IRS) has cautioned that participation in certain managed care contracting joint ventures can jeopardize a hospital's exemption where the capital contributed proportionately outweighs the governance interest retained by the hospital.[12,13] This problem is not erased by section 4041 of the BBA. That section provides that a hospital will not threaten its exemption simply by participating in a PSO. The legislative history of the section makes clear, however, that participation in the entity by the exempt hospital must still meet the rest of the IRS's test for joint ventures (i.e., "whether the sharing of profits and losses or other aspects of the arrangement entail improper private inurement or more than incidental private benefit").[14] Thus, these requirements will effectively preclude a tax-exempt hospital (or group of hospitals) from supplying virtually all of the capital to the PSO for purposes of meeting the solvency requirements while sharing governance on a 50/50 basis with the physicians and other PSO providers.

What Are the Alternatives?

For-Profit Models

Some providers may elect to structure their PSO as either a for-profit stock company or a limited liability company. One advantage of doing this is that the PSO could raise the solvency-required reserves through the sale of stock (in the case of the for-profit corporation) or membership interests (in the case of the limited liability company [LLC]) to a hospital and a larger number of individual physician investors.[15] In this way, the governance of the entity could be structured to conform to the providers' equity contribution, thus eliminating the concern described above for tax-exempt entities that provide disproportionate amounts of capital.

On the other hand, raising the needed solvency capital through the sale of equity interests will demand compliance with federal and state securities laws, requiring appropriate exemptions from registration (assuming the PSO will qualify) and necessary disclosure documents. The compliance effort will add substantially to the transaction costs and time needed to make the PSO operational. Given that current federal waivers from state licensure last for only a three-year period, it is possible that providers may determine that, because of the additional legal constraints, this model is not cost-effective.

The Hospital Subsidiary Model

Given that the hospitals participating in the PSO may be better able to provide the necessary reserve requirements without the need for securities act compliance, providers may want to consider the feasibility of simply structuring the PSO as a wholly-owned subsidiary of the hospital. Under this model, governance would be shared to some degree with the physicians (although the hospital would have to maintain ultimate control of the venture to protect its tax-exempt status, as described above). The statutory requirement of shared financial risk would be met through provider agreements with physicians and other health care professionals. In addition, the fact that a single provider (the hospital) maintained control over the PSO would meet HCFA's requirement that an affiliated provider maintain effective control over the PSO.

It is possible, although perhaps unlikely, for this entity if structured as a nonprofit corporation, to qualify for tax-exempt status. In this event, the tax-exempt hospital could capitalize the new entity and be assured that its provision of the capital would further the hospital's exempt purpose. Arguably, PSOs have a charitable purpose; the IRS has previously recognized that the provision of services to Medicare beneficiaries is a positive factor in securing exemption.[16] Similarly, section 4401 of the BBA recognizes that a PSO's activities can be considered charitable, as the statute expressly recognizes that an exempt hospital does not violate its charitable purpose by participating in such activities. Finally, the legislation itself suggests that PSOs could qualify for exemption.[17]

It is uncertain whether the IRS will accept this position and grant exemption to PSOs structured as controlled subsidiaries of tax-exempt hospitals. The IRS takes an expansive view of section 501(m) of the Internal Revenue Code, which denies exemption, under either sections 501(c)(3) or 501(c)(4), to entities if a substantial part of their activities consists of providing commercial-type insurance. Specifically, in General Counsel Memorandum 39829, the IRS denied exemption to a health maintenance organization (HMO) because its physician provider agreements were deemed to shift risk to the physicians (i.e., the HMO was deemed to be in the insurance business, in violation of Section 501[m]). It is uncertain how the IRS would react to a PSO structure where, by statute, the providers were required to share substantial financial risk and whether this would automatically disqualify the PSO from exemption.

In the event that exemption is not available, the hospital subsidiary could operate either as a wholly owned stock company or a taxable nonprofit corporation, with a shared governance structure as described above. In this event, the sponsors of the PSO should consider whether insurance company taxation (with the associated ability to deduct certain loss reserves) would be available. This strategy, combined with the payment to providers of PSO surplus under the provider agreements, should minimize the PSO's tax liability.

The Physician Entity Model

It is not necessary for hospital providers to own and control PSOs. In fact, it is equally feasible for a physician group practice, (either with or without physician practice management company support), to establish a PSO. In this model, the physician group would establish the PSO as a controlled subsidiary of the group. The group would capitalize the entity with cash sufficient to meet the reserve requirements described above. The PSO would then execute provider agreements with one or more hospitals and physician groups in order to meet the "substantially all" requirement. Hospital guarantees could be used to satisfy any projected shortfalls. Securities issues would be minimized given the smaller number of investors. The "affiliated provider" tests described above would be satisfied through the risk-sharing nature of the provider agreements and the control exercised by the owner physicians.

The Network Model

Another feasible model resembles a combination of the hospital subsidiary and physician entity models described above. In this structure, two or more hospitals, perhaps in combination with two or more physicians groups would establish a jointly owned subsidiary.[18] Each provider would capitalize the entity and receive an equity (or membership) interest in proportion to the capital contributed. Hospital guarantees could be utilized to meet projected shortfalls (as long as the solvency requirements were met). As with the physician equity model, securities issues would be minimized because of the small number of investors. The providers would execute provider agreements with the PSO, allowing them to satisfy the "substantial financial risk" requirements described above.

The Delivery System Model

When provider groups advocated in favor of PSO authorizing legislation, they envisioned a process whereby their delivery system assets (the hospital "bricks and mortar") could be counted toward satisfying the solvency requirements and thus help them to obtain a federal waiver of state licensure requirements.[19] The reality is somewhat different. The solvency rules will allow such assets to be included, but only if they are on the balance sheet of the PSO, thus requiring a problematic transfer of assets from the hospital to the PSO entity.

An IDS, such as an academic medical center that comprises both the hospital component of a delivery system and, through employment contracts, the physician component, could consider using the IDS itself as the PSO (which would function simply as a separate line of business). In this way, the delivery system and the PSO would be one and the same legal entity, and the reserve requirements would be met, in part, through the use of the delivery system assets. Because the services would be provided through a single provider, there would be no need to create "affiliated providers" connected to the PSO through risk-sharing provider agreements.

The solvency rules implicitly recognize this approach, since they allow the PSO to be a component of another legal entity. It is uncertain however whether this structure would qualify for a HCFA waiver of the state licensure requirements. To illustrate, many states require that HMOs be separate legal entities. If a state turned down a PSO license application received from a delivery system PSO structured on this basis because the risk-bearing entity was not a separate legal entity, it is not clear that the license rejection would otherwise entitle the applicant to a federal waiver. Thus, the feasibility of this model—which would make moot many of the issues described above—turns largely on particular state law requirements. Moreover, the continued feasibility of this model at the end of the three-year waiver process also has to be examined, because at that point state licensure again becomes relevant (assuming the waiver period is not extended through legislation).

CONTRACTING CONSIDERATIONS

Once the PSO is established, it will be important (assuming the entity is using an affiliated group of providers) to construct appropriate provider agreements. Although these agreements will resemble provider agreements now used widely today, there are certain key differences that must be planned for.

First, the agreements must use an acceptable risk-sharing mechanism in order to satisfy the requirement that the providers share substantial financial risk. Second, physicians participating in the PSO will be considered to be "insiders" for purposes of determining whether a tax-exempt hospital participant's exemption is in jeopardy.[20] As a practical matter, if the AAPCC payments to the PSO are distributed "too generously" to the physician participants, the hospital could lose its tax exemption. Thus, extreme care needs to be taken when structuring the physician and hospital payment methodologies and risk pools to ensure that the division is supportable.

Finally, the contracts must reflect certain provisions lobbied for by the physician community, including procedures for

> (A) providing notice of the rules regarding [physician] participation,
>
> (B) providing written notice of participation decisions that are adverse to physicians, and
>
> (C) providing a process within the organization for appealing such adverse decisions, including the presentation of information and views of the physician regarding such decisions.[21]

These rules attempt in large measure to end the standard "without cause" termination procedures commonly found in provider agreements, and instead adopt a due process and hearing approach now imposed on managed care plans by various court decisions in California and elsewhere.[22] Thus, provider agreements must be crafted to meet these new and additional requirements.

PSO OPERATIONS

Applicability of State Laws Other than Insolvency Laws

Before turning to a discussion of PSO legal operational issues, it should be noted that FW-PSOs may still be subject to various state law provisions, even if they have received the three-year waiver of state law licensing requirements. According to the BBA, the state solvency licensing requirements still applicable to FW-PSOs will be those that would apply to other Medicare+Choice organizations, are consistent with the new federal standards, and do not relate to the following: benefits requirements, inclusion or treatment of providers, and coverage determinations (including related appeals and grievance processes) (BBA, §1856[b]). The BBA further provides that, during the waiver period, state "consumer protection and quality standards" will apply just as if the PSO were state licensed.

To the extent that FW-PSOs are subject to state law, numerous questions are raised. For example, what kind of jurisdiction, if any, does the state have over FW-PSOs? How will FW-PSOs comply with nonsolvency state laws designed to apply to these types of state-licensed entities, even though the FW-PSO itself is not licensed under state law? Who will enforce PSO compliance with state law, if required? The state? HCFA? The state under contract with HCFA?

HCFA makes an effort to address these issues in the interim final PSO rules. More specifically, § 422.378, which is entitled "Relationship to State Law," provides that the waiver of the state licensure requirement is conditioned upon the organization's compliance with state consumer protection and quality standards that (1) would apply if the organization was licensed under state law; (2) generally apply to other Medicare+Choice organizations and plans in the state; and (3) are consistent with Part C standards. HCFA then states that any such state standards will be incorporated into the FW-PSO's Medicare+Choice contract, and that HCFA *may* enter into an agreement with the state to monitor and enforce compliance with these requirements. Finally, HCFA notes in the preamble to this rule that it is developing a memorandum of understanding with NACC to implement these rules.[23]

Clearly HCFA has recognized that there may be certain state nonsolvency requirements that are not otherwise preempted and which somehow will need to be enforced. Yet the regulatory scheme leaves open many issues. Who will be responsible to make the decision as to which state consumer protection and quality standards apply to FW-PSOs? HCFA? The state? The PSO? Will this be negotiated with the PSO as part of the Medicare+Choice contract? What if the state will not agree to take on the compliance function? Who will pay the state? Will the state report compliance problems to HCFA, or will it have authority to sanction the FW-PSO? Will HCFA have separate authority to review the state's findings (as with the solvency standards), or will it be bound to accept state compliance determinations? How will such determinations impact the renew ability or termination of the Medicare+Choice contract? The complexity of these issues is illustrated by looking at three different types of state laws.

HMO Grievance Procedure Requirements

Many states require licensed HMOs to have grievance procedures for quality of care and for coverage determinations, and some further require that dissatisfied enrollees be able to appeal to an independent third party. Since this is not a solvency requirement, must FW-PSOs comply with these types of state laws applicable to HMOs? The answer is unclear. Clearly these grievance procedures would apply to other Medicare+Choice contractors (i.e., those that are state-licensed), and clearly these procedures are not inconsistent with the BBA. Moreover, while the BBA would preempt state grievance procedures relating to coverage determinations, it would not preempt such procedures as they relate to quality of care decisions. Thus, one reasonable reading of the BBA is that it requires FW-PSOs to comply with state HMO grievance procedure requirements for noncoverage matters. However, from a practical perspective, as noted above, it is not clear under federal or state law exactly how it will be determined which parts of this type of state grievance procedure relate to noncoverage matters. For example, it is not realistic to think that HCFA would render a legal opinion on a state law interpretation.

Other State Licensure Laws Regulating Utilization Review and Third-Party Administrators

In most states with utilization review (UR) and/or third-party administrator (TPA) laws, HMOs or other licensed entities are not required to obtain UR or TPA licenses, at least with respect to their HMO enrollees. These entities are often exempted because these functions are otherwise regulated pursuant to the licensure process. Since these rules do not generally apply to other Medicare+Choice contractors, arguably they should not apply to FW-PSOs. However, by their own terms, these requirements would probably not contain an exception for FW-PSOs. Moreover, the rationale for the exception (i.e., the state already regulates the function) would not be supportable. Thus, FW-PSOs will need to assess whether there are any such other requirements in the state to which they might have to comply. Of course, many of the UR laws, as set forth by their own provisions, do not apply to federal government programs (e.g., peer review organizations are universally exempt from UR laws). Likewise, TPA laws generally apply to those who administer claims on behalf of a "plan sponsor" or "insurer," which would invariably exclude HCFA. However, FW-PSOs will need to review this issue under applicable state law to assess whether any state non-HMO type laws are applicable.

State Consumer Protection Laws

Most states have laws relating to full and fair disclosure to consumers and to protecting consumers from various types of fraud. Generally these laws apply to all businesses, not just health care companies. While it would be expected that any such laws would be applicable to FW-PSOs, it remains to be determined how this would work in practice.

In sum, each FW-PSO must make its own determination as to which other requirements of state law are applicable to its operations. This may prove to be a challenging process and one without much guidance or certainty from either federal or state regulators.

Other Special Treatment of PSOs under the BBA

In addition to the unique federal waiver of state licensure relating to solvency, the BBA provides only one other specific benefit for PSOs. More specifically, PSOs (both FW-PSOs and state-licensed PSOs) may take advantage of a PSO-specific provision regarding minimum enrollment. All Medicare+Choice contractors must meet the requirement for minimum enrollment, which is 5,000 individuals for plans primarily serving persons living in urban areas and 1,500 for plans primarily serving rural areas. The plans must achieve these enrollment levels in order to qualify for the obtainment of a contract. However, for PSOs, these levels are 1,500 or 500, respectively (BBA, §1857[b][1]).

Of course, under Medicare+Choice, HCFA may waive the minimum enrollment requirement during the first three contract years for any organization (BBA, §1857[b][3]). This waiver is available for *any* applicant, not just PSOs. Because most FW-PSOs (which by definition are only eligible to serve Medicare enrollees until they obtain a state license) will not have any enrollment at the time of their application, it would seem likely that they will need to seek the total enrollment waiver and thus would not be in a position to benefit from the reduced minimum enrollment levels for PSOs. On the other hand, the main reason that a state-licensed PSO may want to be officially designated as a PSO by HCFA would be to qualify for the reduced minimum enrollment threshold. This would be particularly true for new plans that have some enrollment (e.g., the sponsor hospital's own employees) but not enough to meet the urban or rural level. Whether a PSO seeks official designation may also depend to some extent on whether the entity determines that it would be easier to meet the PSO definition requirements (thereby qualifying for the lower enrollment threshold) or seek the three-year total waiver available for all plans. It is not yet clear what that waiver process will involve, but it is likely that HCFA will be reluctant to make total enrollment waivers readily available. HCFA's concern, of course, will be that the solvency of a plan with few or no enrollees will be jeopardized if the plan has one or a few very high-cost enrollees. At a minimum, it can be expected that, as part of any such waiver, HCFA would require plans to have greater financial reserves and additional financial protections to compensate for the lack of other sources of income.

It also should be noted that the value of being able to qualify for the PSO minimum enrollment threshold may depend on how HCFA defines "enrollment" for purposes of this requirement. Section 1857(b)(1)(A) of the BBA provides that a PSO must have at least 1,500 individuals "who are receiving health benefits through the organization." Interestingly, this terminology is different from that of the current rule for risk contractors, which requires 5,000 commercial "enrollees" (42 CFR §417.413[b] and Medicare CMP Manual §2000). It is possible that HCFA will determine that an entity that, through a "global" or full-risk contract, assumes the responsibility to provide or arrange for care of enrollees in a state-licensed health plan could be allowed to count those "delegated" lives toward meeting the "minimum enrollment" levels as defined in the BBA. Thus, a PSO that subcontracted with a health plan to provide care to the health plan's enrollees (which arrangement does not require a license in most states) might be able to count those persons toward meeting the minimum enrollment threshold and thus not need a total waiver of the minimum enrollment requirement.

As a related matter, it should be noted that the Medicare 50/50 enrollment composition rule will be repealed effective January 1, 1999, for all plans, so the requirement that the enrollees be *commercial* for purposes of meeting the minimum levels (in contrast to individuals covered under any health coverage, including Medicaid) will no longer be an issue for state-licensed PSOs or FW-PSOs or for any other contractor. Perhaps the more significant issue for PSOs is whether HCFA, in Part C rule making, will repeal the current requirement that prohibits plans from having Medicare-only providers (Medicare CMP Manual §2160.1 and §2303.1[B]). If not, HCFA will need to make some exception for FW-PSOs that are serving only the Medicare population and whose providers, by definition, are Medicare-only providers.

Applicability of Other Medicare Requirements to PSO Operations

Perhaps the most significant factor to keep in mind regarding legal issues is that PSOs are essentially Medicare health plans and must comply with all Medicare contract laws, rules, policies, and guidelines unless such requirements specifically exempt

PSOs. While a lot of attention has been paid to establishing PSOs and obtaining appropriate licensure (whether state or federal), potentially the most difficult legal issues facing a PSO will arise in its conducting of business as a Medicare health plan. The Medicare risk business that PSOs are entering is in the process of becoming much more regulated, with more federal oversight, more data requirements, more quality and quality improvement obligations, more compliance activity, more beneficiary advocacy involvement, more fraud and abuse oversight, and generally much greater scrutiny. There is no reason to believe that any of this scrutiny will be reduced for PSOs; indeed in many arenas, as discussed below, the compliance burdens may be even greater for PSOs.

The key requirements for Medicare+Choice organizations are as follows:

- They must assume full financial risk but may obtain stop-loss insurance and/or capitate providers to assume all or part of the risk for services provided by or through these providers (§1855[b]).
- They must accept any Medicare member who is eligible to elect the plan, unless the number of eligible individuals electing the plan exceeds the plan's capacity as determined by HCFA (§1851[g]).
- They must provide all basic benefits to members, which include all items and services available under traditional Medicare plus benefits, in a value equal to the difference between the average capitation payments to the plan and the plan's adjusted community rate.
- They must accept as payment in full the Medicare capitation rates.
- They must comply with all marketing, enrollment, disenrollment, appeals and grievance, provider contracting, and other rules.

The areas that may pose potential difficulties for PSO compliance are discussed below.

Marketing

HCFA has issued "Medicare Managed Care National Marketing Guidelines," which describe the dos and don'ts of plan marketing.[24] The guidelines (which are available on the Internet at the HCFA website) are designed primarily to assist with the preapproval of marketing materials and secondarily as a policy reference source for marketing activities. From a compliance perspective, HCFA treats the guidelines as mandatory rules.

The guidelines define providers very broadly, to include any entity in a plan's network, and then they address provider promotional activities. More specifically, HCFA states that it strongly discourages provider marketing because providers are not usually fully aware of membership plan benefits and costs; beneficiaries may be confused as to when the providers are acting as plan agents; and providers' knowledge of their patients' health status increases the potential for their discriminating in favor of Medicare beneficiaries with a positive health status when acting as marketing agents.[25] However, recognizing marketplace realities, HCFA does provide a fairly narrow set of permissible provider marketing activities, including handing out brochures, cosponsoring events with a health plan, announcing new affiliations with a health plan, and furnishing a health plan a complete list of patients' names.

The area of provider marketing will likely pose difficulties for PSOs, since the providers are both the owners of and contract providers to the plan. What is permissible for providers in one role (e.g., the ownership role) may be completely in conflict with what is permissible in the other role (the care provision role). For example, the rules on announcing a new affiliation state that "an announcement of a new affiliation provider, naming only one plan to a patient, may occur only once. Additional marketing contacts with the provider's patients must include information on all Medicare plans with which the provider contracts."[26] As applied to PSOs, it could mean that, after the first announcement of the provider's affiliation with the PSO, any further announcement must include all

Medicare+Choice contractors with which the provider contracts, not just the PSO. Moreover, as discussed in the fraud and abuse section below, PSOs will run the risk that their affiliated providers will use knowledge of their patients' health status in determining whether to encourage these beneficiaries to enroll. Thus, it is not clear how PSOs, which by definition are owned and controlled by providers, will be legally able to conduct effective marketing within the parameters of the guidelines. At a minimum, HCFA may need to revise the guidelines to address permissible PSO marketing activity.

Encounter Data Risk Adjustors

Under the BBA, the Department of Health and Human Services (DHHS) is required to implement a risk-adjustment methodology that accounts for variation in per capita costs based on health status. This payment method must be implemented no later than January 1, 2000, and shall apply to all types of plans. As part of this initiative, the BBA requires all Medicare+Choice organizations to submit encounter data. Data regarding inpatient hospital services are required for discharges on or after July 1, 1997. HCFA began requiring collection of these data starting January 1, 1998. Other data on all other services will be required beginning July 1, 1998. HCFA currently is developing its requirements for the collection of encounter data.

These are significant data collection obligations, which require the plans, including PSOs, to carefully monitor provider compliance. The managed care industry as a whole is extremely concerned about this initiative for many reasons. One worry is that HCFA encounter data will not pick up non-Medicare benefits whose use may lead to reductions in hospital encounters, such as prescription drug benefits. A more general worry is that the whole initiative could be viewed as a return to a cost utilization–based system, which would totally defeat the purpose of managed care. The initiative may make the business of operating PSOs even more speculative. Since PSOs are likely to have smaller enrollments, at least initially, the risk adjustors could vary payment more significantly and have a major impact on financial viability. Moreover, depending on how the risk adjustors are implemented, it is unclear how PSOs will be able to meet the requirement that their affiliated providers be at substantial financial risk.

Physician Incentive Plan Rules

The physician incentive plan (PIP) rules at 42 CFR §417.479 require that if plans place physicians at substantial financial risk, as defined by the regulations, this information must be disclosed to HCFA and to beneficiaries, and appropriate stop-loss must be provided. The industry has faced serious issues regarding the PIP rules, including the definition of substantial financial risk, the ability of plans to ascertain how individual physicians are paid, and the difficulty and expense of obtaining the required stop-loss insurance. The PIP substantial financial risk regulations, in many instances, have been deemed to impede the ability of managed care plans to structure payment arrangements the way they would like. The definition of substantial financial risk used in applying the PIP rules is not the same as that used to determine if providers have assumed sufficient financial risk to be considered affiliates of the PSO. However, physicians who are PSO affiliates (and therefore are at significant financial risk) will probably satisfy the substantial financial risk definition used in the PIP rules. Based on this assumption, PSOs will likely face the same types of PIP compliance questions as health plans: Who will pay for the stop-loss? What do you disclose to beneficiaries about how physicians are paid? How can you protect the confidentiality of specific physician payments rates?

Moreover, PSOs may face the very significant problem that the stop-loss provisions strongly discourage placing physicians at substantial financial risk until there are at least 500 enrollees that are subject to the stop-loss pool. For many start-up PSOs, it will likely be at least a year before the 500 threshold is met. Thus, PSOs may find themselves in the untenable position of being required by one set of rules to have affiliated physicians at substantial financial risk and at the same time being strongly discouraged by another set of rules from placing the physicians at substantial financial risk.

ACR Calculations

Each Medicare+Choice contractor is required to submit adjusted community rate (ACR) filings to determine how much extra benefits need to be provided to the its Medicare enrollees. The ACRs basically reflect the plan's costs in providing services to non-Medicare enrollees. Yet, PSOs by definition will not have an enrolled non-Medicare population on which to base the ACR. The BBA provides that, for all new plans, including PSOs, HCFA can determine the ACR based on the enrollment experience of other contractors and may use rates from the general commercial marketplace to calculate an ACR for a particular PSO (§1854[f][4]). However, there is no requirement that the rate be from a comparable marketplace for a specific PSO or that HCFA negotiate or even discuss the ACR calculation with the PSO. It could be very difficult, at least initially, to ensure that an appropriate ACR calculation is being applied for any particular PSO, and the PSO's ability to control its product, premium structure, and benefits could be substantially reduced. How HCFA elects to determine the ACR for new PSOs could become a significant issue.

Employer Group Agreements

Many risk contractors find an attractive part of their Medicare book of business is retirees covered under employer group retiree arrangements. While these beneficiaries still enroll in Medicare health plans under individual policies, the plans and employers often enter into arrangements pursuant to which the employer pays an additional premium to add additional benefits for the retiree. HCFA does not really regulate these arrangements as long as the individual receives extra benefits from the group; the benefits package cannot in any way reduce the benefits to which the individual would otherwise be entitled.[27]

Employer group retiree arrangements raise several interesting issues for PSOs. The first is whether federally waived PSOs are legally authorized to enter into contracts with employers. The BBA specifically authorizes PSOs only to enter into Medicare+Choice contracts with HCFA. To the extent that the employer agreement serves solely to add benefits for Medicare enrollees under Medicare+Choice, arguably PSOs should be able to enter into such arrangements and 42 CFR § 422.375 would preempt any state effort to regulate these arrangements. However, to the extent that the PSO is promising to cover all of a specified benefit package (e.g., pharmacy) in exchange for a monthly premium, it is reasonable to conclude that a state insurance regulator could deem that coverage to be the business of insurance, which requires state licensure.

A related issue for federally waived PSOs is how and when HCFA will implement § 1851(c)(3) of the BBA. This allows HCFA to develop a process under which a working person who (a) is covered under a health plan that is also a Medicare+Choice contractor; (b) ages into Medicare; and (c) does not otherwise select another plan will be automatically deemed to have elected to stay in the plan in which they are enrolled under Medicare+Choice. Once implemented, this could be a significant boon to Medicare+Choice contracts with large commercial contracts and a significant impediment to PSOs that will not be able to take advantage of this "deeming" process. Thus, the Medicare-only focus of PSOs may in fact be a detriment to PSOs seeking to increase their enrollment.

Fraud and Abuse

Generally the fraud and abuse health care regulators have been increasingly concerned about compliance by Medicare managed care contractors. One worrisome issue is the potential for "steerage" or "cherry picking," which is where a plan seeks, by any number of means, to try to get healthier beneficiaries to enroll in the plan and to dissuade less healthy individuals (high utilizers of services) from enrolling or to encourage them to disenroll. This problem is exacerbated in the case of PSOs, since the providers have access to member health status information. Indeed, HCFA already has stated that PSOs can expect much closer fraud and abuse scrutiny because they are in a position to "health screen" potential enrollees. The sanctions, including the imposition of significant civil monetary penalties, available to HCFA and to the DHHS Office of the Inspector General (OIG) are broad and far ranging.

Moreover, for PSOs in particular, another problem in the fraud and abuse arena is that the various fraud and abuse statutes and regulations invariably fail to mention or acknowledge the existence of PSOs. For example, the proposed Stark II rules (63 *Fed. Reg.* 1659 et. seq, January 9, 1998) contain limited exceptions from both the ownership and compensation prohibitions for certain types of prepaid health plans and physician incentive plans. The only prepaid health plans enumerated in the statute are Medicare risk contracting HMOs, health care prepayment plans, plans operated under demonstration projects, and federally qualified HMOs. In the proposed Stark II rules, HCFA expands this list to Medicaid risk contracting HMOs under the Medicaid program. Neither the statute nor the proposed Stark II rules would protect financial interests in other forms of prepaid health plans, including HMOs that are federally qualified or any form of PSO or for that matter any Medicare+Choice contractor. While a detailed review of Stark II implications for managed care plans is beyond the scope of this chapter, suffice it to say that PSOs do not fall under any Stark exception.

Similarly, HCFA and the OIG are currently developing separate rules through a negotiated rulemaking process to implement the section of the Health Insurance Portability Accountability Act of 1996 (HIPPA) that also provides managed care risk-sharing exceptions from the general Medicare/Medicaid fraud and abuse laws. The draft of HIPPA rules, which are expected to be published in the near future, is viewed by some as flawed in terms of protecting many of the common types of risk-incentive arrangements used by managed care companies. More significantly, they, like the Stark rules, do not address or provide any guidance as to how PSOs might fit into a managed care safe harbor. Thus, like all other players in the health arena today, PSOs are going to have to keep a very careful eye on their operations to guard against fraud and abuse exposure.

CONCLUSION

PSOs face many legal challenges, both in their establishment and their operations as Medicare+Choice contractors. In many ways, despite the regulatory uncertainties, setting up a PSO will likely be easier than operating the business while staying in compliance with applicable laws. Some of the challenges can be identified now; others will only emerge as HCFA issues new rules and policies and as providers attempt to work through the numerous issues that arise out of their need to function as both owners and providers. The potential for conflicts of interest in these roles, the difficulties facing PSOs in accessing employees as they become retirees, as well as the increased regulatory oversight over Medicare managed care, will possibly make it even harder to operate as a PSO than another type of Medicare health plan.

NOTES

1. Other legal issues, such as what state actions are sufficient to trigger the federal waiver process, are discussed elsewhere in this book.
2. For example, there has been some discussion that HCFA may want the ability to terminate PSOs more quickly than other health plan contractors.
3. "Substantial proportion" is defined as at least 70 percent of the Medicare services provided under the contract (except that for rural PSOs, this requirement is lowered to 60 percent). 63 Fed. Reg. 18135 (April 14, 1998).
4. 63 Fed. Reg. 18134 (April 14, 1998).
5. Ibid.
6. Section 1563 applies only to for-profit, stock corporations and generally treats corporations as controlled groups where one owns the stock of another (parent-subsidiary relationship) or the same individuals own the stock of two or more corporations (brother-sister relationship).

7. Section 414(m) utilizes the concept of an "affiliated services group." This concept is applicable in cases where different employers are treated as a single employer for benefits and testing purposes if certain ownership and business relationships exist between the two. An affiliated service group relationship generally will not exist (other than in the case where an entity provides certain management services) without common ownership.
8. 63 Fed. Reg. 18135 (April 14, 1998).
9. Ibid at 18133.
10. 42 U.S.C. §1857(b)(3).
11. *See generally*, 63 Fed. Reg. 25360-25379 (May 7, 1998).
12. "Can a PHO Threaten a Hospital's Tax Exempt Status?" Healthcare Financial Management 21 (July 1994):
13. Internal Revenue Service, *Continuing Technical Instruction Program Textbook*, part 2 (Washington, DC: Internal Revenue Service, 1995), chap. P, pp. 19.
14. Conference Report, 694.
15. In our view, the LLC form does not offer significant advantages over a for-profit corporation. Although the LLC in theory eliminates one layer of tax (at the entity level), taxes at the PSO level should not be of concern, given the likelihood of losses in the start-up period and the ability of the PSO to pay out the PSO's surplus to the providers pursuant to their provider agreements.
16. Rev. Rul. 69-545.
17. Section 4401 of the BBA contains the phrase "whether or not the [PSO] is exempt from tax."
18. This model could be structured as a for-profit stock company, LLC, or non-profit membership corporation.
19. Conference Report, 636.
20. See BBA, §4041(a), which adds a new subsection (o) to Section 501 of the Internal Revenue Code.
21. 42 U.S.C. §1852(j).
22. *See generally*, "Terminating Physicians in Managed Care Organizations," Healthcare Financial Management 31 (January 1998).
23. Fed. Reg. 25364.
24. The guidelines were released on September 8, 1997, and were last updated on November 14, 1997.
25. Ibid., p. 27.
26. Ibid.
27. HCFA Operational Policy Letter #27.

CHAPTER 5

Financial Considerations for Provider Sponsored Organizations

Daniel M. Scheibenreif

The prospect of accepting risk for a population of covered lives opens a whole new world of opportunities for provider sponsored organizations (PSOs). Along with these new opportunities comes a host of financial challenges and considerations that every successful PSO will need to address.

This chapter presents a general PSO financial model. While each PSO will have unique characteristics, features, and objectives that distinguish it from other PSOs in the marketplace, the general model can be used to illustrate and frame discussions of various financial parameters that are central to designing and maintaining provider-based organizations.

GENERAL FINANCIAL MODEL

Figure 5–1 illustrates the general PSO financial model. The various levels of the model and the financial issues that relate to each are discussed below.

The Covered Membership

The top level of the model indicates the most common reason the PSO providers have come together: to care for a population of patients.

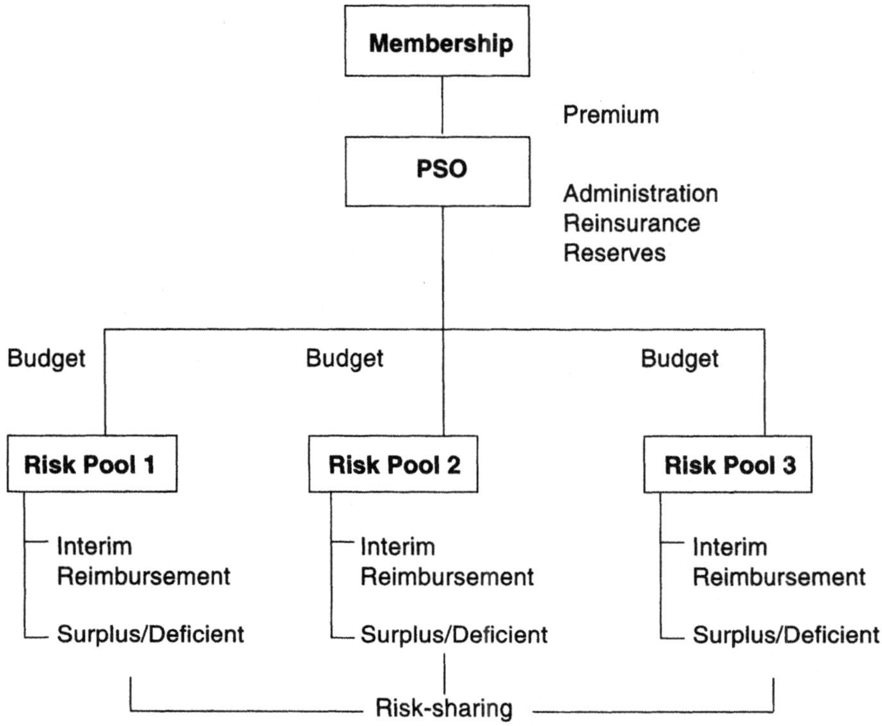

Figure 5–1 PSO financial model.

In the case of most PSOs (especially those set up as physician hospital organizations [PHOs]), the membership has been delivered through capitated arrangements (often capitation) with health plans (health maintenance organizations [HMOs]) licensed to market products in the area. Occasionally, a PSO will also derive membership through a subcontract with another provider organization wishing to expand its service area or extend the scope of patient care services it offers.

A third means by which a PSO can develop a membership base is through direct contracting with government programs as well as the retiree population of large employers. For many newer PSOs serving rural areas that have not been attractive enough to HMOs looking for business, this may be the only means. Existing PHOs, independent practitioner associations (IPAs), and other integrated provider systems want to open up the direct channel, since it effectively removes the health plan (and its layer of profit and administrative expenses) from the system. Regulatory restrictions and marketplace realities have kept the direct contracting pipeline from opening up, but changes introduced by the Balanced Budget Act of 1997 should result in more direct contracting opportunities. PSOs that are able to manage risk in this new environment successfully will actively seek new business and can be in a position to effectively compete with HMOs in the area, with the advantage of local name recognition.

The PSO

At the second level of the financial model is the PSO itself. Premium revenue flows into the PSO from health plan capitation agreements and direct contracts with government programs. The PSO's expenses include the cost of administrative/management services, reinsurance, and patient care services by providers.

Since, over the long term, provider reimbursement rates will be governed by the amount of available revenue, the PSO leadership should address a key financial and strategic consideration early on in the planning and development stage: what is the minimum revenue rate that is consistent with the PSO's objectives? Too often, provider organizations are formed and become operational before they define (or even consider) this "walk-away" revenue level. Without such a benchmark for contracting, it is quite easy for the PSO to allow market forces, rather than financial discipline, to determine which contracts are accepted. Minimum revenue rates should be established by type of contract (commercial, Medicare, Medicaid), with the ability to adjust the targets based on variations in plan design (e.g., copays, exclusions, and maximums) and demographic mix (age and gender). The walk-away revenue level is an especially important consideration when the PSO accepts percentage-of-premium risk contracts. Establishing, negotiating, and enforcing revenue floors helps avoid the situation where a health plan builds market share by aggressively cutting premium rates and effectively placing a portion of the premium reduction on the back of the PSO.

Reinsurance contracts are used to protect the PSO from large adverse fluctuations in claims. This protection can come in the form of specific reinsurance, aggregate reinsurance, or both.

Specific reinsurance protects the organization from the impact of high-cost individuals. For example, coverage terms might be stated as 50-percent coinsurance in excess of a $25,000 per member deductible. There may be separate agreements covering hospital and physician services or a single contract that includes all patient care. Specific protection, typically quoted as a per member per month (PMPM) amount, may be built into a payer agreement or may be obtained separately from a commercial reinsurance carrier.

Aggregate reinsurance protects the PSO from unusually high claim levels across the entire covered population. A typical aggregate stop-loss contract covers a portion of excess claims once they exceed a stated percentage (e.g., 120 percent) of a predefined "expected" claim level. The need for aggregate protection is lessened by the presence of specific coverage with low deductibles, but aggregate coverage should still be considered as a tool for financial management. Aggregate reinsurance has been provided to provider organizations primarily through risk-sharing thresholds (e.g., fee-for-service guarantees). As the PSO market expands, reinsurance carriers will likely respond with more access to traditional aggregate reinsurance contracts.

Reinsurance premiums are often treated as an administrative cost, and any claims recovered can be treated as supplemental income to offset provider expenses. Alternatively, the cost of reinsurance and the resulting recoveries can be allocated to the provider pools. The PSO leadership should consider the degree of financial variation that is acceptable and obtain reinsurance contracts that are consistent with this risk tolerance.

Additional amounts may also be set aside for reserves. These reserves would normally be established to provide a buffer from adverse fluctuations in experience. To some extent, such contingency reserves and reinsurance coverage achieve much the same objective. The appropriate amount of the reserves will be influenced by the applicable statutory surplus requirements.

The Provider Network

At the third level of the financial model is the provider network. Typically, provider networks are separated into pools that are funded by the PSO with a fixed (capitated) or target (budgeted) revenue amount. The pools may be set up in several ways: by provider type, as in a PHO (institutional and professional or institutional, primary care, and specialist); by clinical department, as in the case of academic health centers; or integrated into a single pool. PSOs in rural areas with limited access to newer treatments and technology might also consider a separate pool for referral and tertiary care that may be directed to larger hospitals or academic health centers. Special pools may also be defined for specific conditions such as asthma and diabetes. An illustrative pooling structure is provided in Table 5–1.

Once the pools have been defined, the PSO needs to determine the interim reimbursement mechanisms that govern the purchasing of health care services. Each of the pools may bear financial responsibility for health services that use various types of reimbursement mechanisms. The establishment of a reimbursement mechanism for each type of service involves two

Table 5–1 Sample Risk Pool Structure

Pool	*Services*
Institutional	Inpatient, outpatient surgery facility, outpatient treatments (rehab, dialysis, etc.), emergency department facility, ambulance, home health
Physician	Primary care, referral physician, surgeon, hospital-based physician, office and outpatient diagnostics
Drugs and other	Prescription drugs, medical equipment, prosthetics

basic parameters: the level of payment and the method of payment. The level of payment must be set high enough to give providers an incentive to participate but low enough to ensure pools do not have more projected expenses than revenue. The method of payment will often take a variety of forms. These forms, in increasing order of provider risk, are described below. Most PSOs will use a combination of them.

Discounted Charges

Although used less frequently, discounts from billed charges still exist in many situations. The primary advantages of charge-based reimbursement are simplicity and ease of implementation. The chief drawbacks of this structure are that it does little to encourage efficient resource utilization, offers little protection against high-cost providers, and makes it difficult to control the year-to-year increases in costs. The structure is most often used in limited situations, such as when more advanced reimbursement structures cannot be applied or where supply and demand forces dictate charge-based methodologies.

Scheduled Fees

Fee schedules, often used for interim payments to specialist physicians and surgical centers, are a form of prospective fee-for-service payment mechanism—providers receive a predefined payment for each procedure or service performed. Although many physicians may prefer this type of methodology, it does little to encourage efficient resource utilization.

Most fee schedules work similarly. There are two basic types—fixed amount schedules and relative value schedules. Fixed amount schedules simply assign each procedure a dollar value, such as $20.00 for a 99211 office visit. In a relative value schedule, each procedure is assigned a unit value intended to reflect the relative value of the procedure. The unit values are then transformed into a fixed-dollar schedule by one or more conversion factors. For example, a resource based relative value system (RBRVS) schedule using a conversion factor of $40.00 would limit payment to $15.20 for procedure code 99211 (the unit value [0.38] times the conversion factor [$40.00] equals the schedule amount [$15.20]).

The actual payment for a service is generally the lesser of the schedule or the billed charge. The PSO or physician network will tend to realize more "salvage" savings (payment reductions from application of the "lesser of" rule) when the fee schedule level is higher relative to billed charges. Conversely, as the effective discount implicit within a fee schedule gets deeper, salvage savings tend to diminish.

There are several common physician fee schedules. Some that enjoy widespread use are the California Relative Values Study (CRVS), St. Anthony's Relative Values for Physicians (formerly published by McGraw-Hill), and Medicare's RBRVS. The RBRVS schedule (with adjustments to increase the schedule and to fill in procedures that are missing, such as laboratory services) probably has had the most widespread use since it was introduced in the early 1990s. For hospital services, Medicare's ambulatory surgical center schedule, modifications of the RBRVS schedule and the Medicare lab fee schedule (for the technical component of diagnostic services), and per diems (for inpatient care) are commonly used.

Episodic or Case Rates

Another approach that has seen growth involves the use of case rates, also referred to as global fees or package pricing. This approach, used frequently for maternity and cardiac care services, among others, may integrate hospital and physician reimbursement and may involve multiple encounters under a single prospectively determined fee.

Under case rates, the PSO retains the risk of a given condition occurring, while the pool assumes the intensity risk—the number and type of services and resources each case requires. The definition of services to be included in a case rate obviously needs to be carefully drafted.

Capitation

In contrast to fee-for-service methods, capitation contracts pay providers a fixed PMPM amount regardless of utilization. This strategy maximizes the incentive for providers to control utilization. Under capitation, providers exchange collection and cash flow risk for utilization risk. Capitated providers expand their role in the health system beyond delivery to become partners in the financing of the system.

In defining a capitation rate, it is first necessary to define the panel of health care services included in the capitation. This is not always simple. Many services, such as office visits, are performed by a wide variety of providers. Therefore, even after the services included in the capitation are defined, a referral authorization system may be needed to review the services performed outside the cap. Furthermore, the set of services under capitation tends to evolve over time. After the services included are defined, a PMPM capitation rate is set based on the expected utilization of services and the target reimbursement per service. Consideration may also be given to competitive capitation rates that are already in place. Capitation rates often are adjusted by age and gender. Capitations can also be coupled with bonus or incentive pools.

The use of specialty capitation has expanded substantially since the early 1990s. Specialty capitation contracts are more difficult to develop and administer. First, a mechanism needs to be developed to allocate covered individuals to a specific specialist or medical group. This can be done by using a single group of specialists for all services or by making the patient or the primary care provider choose a panel of specialists responsible for all their services. Regulatory restrictions may also interfere with the operation of specialty capitation, such as mandates requiring that health plans allow adult female members to choose and access their own ob/gyn physician without prior authorization from the primary care provider.

The Surplus/Deficit Settlement

The last level of the model encompasses the distribution of remaining pool balances among risk pools and the distribution of funds to provider participants in those pools. Completing the design details of this process can easily become the most difficult and complicated part of building the financial model. Since this step requires the provider components to agree on a system for dividing the same dollar of income, a "win" for one part of the network often is seen as a "loss" for the others. A sound rationale that ties the settlement formula to specific criteria or measures helps minimize the impact of these wedges. The PSO leadership should consider the source of the surpluses and deficits and design the disbursement system so that the financial results (good or bad) are aligned with the reimbursement policy that leads to these results.

For example, if market forces result in specialist interim payments that are set at liberal fee-for-service levels with no risk, they probably should draw a lower portion of the surplus, since they received more of the available revenue during the year on a guaranteed basis. Likewise, the PSO hospital may accept a lower interim DRG payment rate with the understanding (and expectation) that it will participate in a greater percentage of the surplus earned during the year.

The pool payouts can also be coupled with contingent performance measurements. Typical measures might include hospital utilization (e.g., percentage of medically unnecessary days), overall cost levels, patient satisfaction scores, and utilization review compliance. PSOs should attempt to allocate this compensation as equitably as possible without overrewarding providers with high utilization levels. However, the allocation process always involves a balancing act—rewarding those with favorable experience while avoiding unduly punishing those who have had poorer experience due to high-risk patients or chance fluctuations.

Finally, there may be a risk-sharing formula for transferring portions of each pool's surplus or deficit to the other pools. Such formulas provide a flexible mechanism for spreading gains and losses across the delivery system, since the percentages assigned to each pool can be changed as circumstances warrant. For example, if the ultimate goal of the PSO is to have each pool assume sole responsibility for the associated health care services, this structure can be used as a way to transition the organization toward that goal.

An illustrative risk-sharing matrix is provided in Table 5–2. Note, in particular, that the sum of the illustrated allocations for the institutional surplus is less than 100 percent. In this example, 10 percent (100 percent minus 50 percent minus 20 percent minus 20 percent) of the institutional pool surplus is retained as a buffer for adverse experience in future years.

In solidifying the details underneath the surplus/deficit settlement process, the PSO leadership will need to address several key considerations. When, and how often, will the settlements be performed? Ideally, the reward for efficient resource usage should be paid out soon after the close of the experience period over which performance was measured in order to reinforce the link between effective performance and financial reward. Unfortunately, this rarely is possible due to the time lag in reporting encounters and adjudicating claims. Settlements that are derived soon after the end of the experience period will need to include provisions for unprocessed claims (often mislabeled "incurred but not reported") and may then require a subsequent "true up" after more time has passed.

The question of how often to calculate and distribute settlements is more difficult. Historically, health plans have maintained incentive and bonus programs on an annual basis to minimize the administrative burden. The PSO may opt to measure surpluses more frequently to keep incentives prominently displayed and thus continually motivate providers to use resources efficiently.

What level of withhold is necessary to ensure that, if experience is less favorable than expected, risk pools will be able to meet the associated obligations? The answer to this question depends on the financial arrangement between the pools and

Table 5–2 Sample Risk-sharing Matrix

Pool	*Hospital Share*	*PCP Share*	*Specialist Share*
Institutional	50%	20%	20%
Physician	0%	50%	50%
Drugs and other	10%	50%	40%

the PSO. For example, if surpluses in other pools will be available to offset deficits in one pool, the withhold required might be minimal or zero. Conversely, if no such surpluses will be available and the PSO must finance pool deficits, a larger withhold might be appropriate.

CONCLUSION

The general financial model presented in this chapter provides a template for addressing the many important financial considerations that will face a new PSO. By addressing these issues early in the planning process, the PSO can direct its resources to accomplishing its objectives.

The landscape of the health care system is continually changing. Financial arrangements and incentive programs—even those designed and implemented with broad acceptance—should be reviewed periodically as regulatory and marketplace dynamics alter the business environment. Establishing mechanisms that are flexible and scaleable makes periodic reviews more manageable.

Chapter 6

Building Value and Core Competencies: Responding to Regulatory and Consumer Demands

Michael Treash and Michele Manfreda

Why is it that providers intent on direct contracting with Medicare to avoid the health maintenance organization (HMO) middleman are essentially copying the HMO's business design? This is the same business design that consumers, legislators, and the press criticize for infringing on patient rights. They use it partially because managed care is driving value in the market right now and partially because Medicare requires private health plans contracting at risk to have managed care processes in place. However, in order for provider sponsored organizations (PSOs) to be successful in the market, they need to focus more on what will deliver value in the future and build competencies around those drivers. The biggest opportunity for PSOs may be provided by the growing consumer movement in health care and by their ability to respond to the market and public policy drivers of consumerism in health care.

This chapter discusses how federal policy is impacting consumer regulation and what it means competitively for PSOs; how the federal government enforces Medicare regulations that pertain to managed care organizations; the Medicare+Choice application process; and the Medicare+Choice regulatory requirements.

PUBLIC POLICY AND HEALTH CARE MARKET FAILURES

Federal policy makers, for nearly three decades, have been confounded by the imperfect market conditions in health care. Calls for national health insurance have been and are today based on the belief that true market conditions are not achievable in health care. Managed competition theorists value the competitive incentives of the market but realize there is a need for government regulation to overcome its deficiencies. Policy makers agree on the challenges of creating marketlike conditions in health care, including the following:

- *Information asymmetry.* Patients do not have sufficient information to make informed decisions about their health care options and as a result rely on providers to make informed decisions on their behalf.
- *Pareto principle.* Payment for service by a third-party payer, such as an insurance company, creates few economic incentives for patients to act like disciplined consumers, especially when an employer provides extensive coverage. Health care virtually becomes a free good.
- *Supplier-induced demand.* Since providers both diagnose and treat, they in essence control both supply and demand.
- *Technology-driven inflation.* Cost increases are driven by technological advancements and incentives to purchase and use the latest medical technologies.
- *Information on providers.* Patients lack sufficient information on the quality or competence of their providers.
- *Uninsured population.* The market has failed to provide universal health insurance coverage, and there are incentives for people to avoid health insurance.

In 1973, policy makers turned aside calls for national health insurance even though they recognized that health care costs were being driven up by the failures of the market. Instead, they looked for market-based solutions. In order to infuse discipline into health care and focus incentives more on patient responsibility and preventive care, the federal government passed legislation to promote the growth of health maintenance organizations. The HMO Act of 1973 helped lower barriers to market entry for these organizations. This act created a federal qualification process that provided the federal government's seal of approval on participating HMOs, required employers to offer an HMO option, and created a loan program to provide seed money for HMO start-ups.

In 1992, federal health care policy came back into the national spotlight with the Clinton health care reform plan. Policy makers recognized that the old deficiencies in the market still existed while new public policy concerns had emerged with the growth of managed care. The new set of health care market issues included these:

- *Access to care.* Concern about quality of care and patient rights arose because of managed care's practice of limiting provider choice and controlling referrals for specialty care.
- *Information on health plans.* This constitutes another element of the information asymmetry. Consumers have little comparative information allowing them to make informed decisions when selecting a health plan.
- *Risk selection.* Managed care's limits on choice and control of access to care may cause sicker individuals to avoid or disenroll from HMOs in favor of traditional fee-for-service plans, thereby increasing the degree of risk selection and the costs of indemnity insurance.

The failure of the Clinton reform plan, because the old and new market unresolved problems were left unresolved, paved the way for the current phase of health care reform efforts. Today, there exists a number of federal and state legislative initiatives aimed at addressing these problems through fostering the growth of a specific social and market force: consumerism. While not a panacea, policy makers view consumerism in health care as a vibrant trend that will significantly reshape the health care marketplace and cause the same outcome that it has in other industries—a centering of the market around the consumer.

REGULATION OF MANAGED CARE ORGANIZATIONS

Regulators, in the case of Medicare+Choice, Congress making laws, and the Health Care Financing Administration (HCFA) creating rules, have at their disposal different types of enforcement capabilities including:

Economic Enforcement

Economic enforcement is the traditional method of government regulation—setting conditions for market entry, establishing consumer protections, and enforcing those requirements. Consumer protection is the primary goal of this type of regulation. Health plans contracting with federal programs are subject to participation requirements similar to those required by state regulators (see Exhibit 6–1). When applying for a Medicare or Medicaid contract, the health plan must meet basic market entry requirements and thereafter ongoing managed care regulations that ensure consumer protection. Additionally, policy makers can regulate the market itself to help ensure access to health insurance by establishing price controls, placing restrictions on rating methods, or creating incentives to serve underserved market segments.

Private Enforcement

Regulation, through private enforcement, allows consumers to seek legal action against a health plan that violates public policy. Private enforcement policy starts with a clearly defined public statement of consumer rights, like the Health Care Con-

Exhibit 6–1 Economic Regulation in the Medicare+Choice Program

Market Entry
- Capitalization
- Management Experience
- Information Management

Financial Solvency
- Net Worth
- Financial Risk Management
- Consumer Insolvency Protection

Managed Care Processes
- Network Management
- Quality Assurance
- Utilization Management
- Marketing and Sales
- Member Services
- Claims and Appeals

Oversight and Enforcement
- Monitoring
- Intermediate Sanctions
  1. Corrective Actions
  2. Fines
  3. Freeze on Enrollment
- Contract Termination
- Civil and Criminal Penalties

Payment
- Geographic Payment Incentives
- Risk Adjustors
- Performance-based Incentives (Future?)

Courtesy of Ernst & Young LLP, Chicago, Illinois.

sumer Bill of Rights. The consumer must have a clear method for appealing to the health plan to reconsider a policy decision and, if not satisfied, must have the ability to file legal action. Consumer groups are pushing for an "enterprise liability" public policy for HMOs, which would hold HMOs responsible not only for their actions but for their policies as well. Recent examples of the increased recognition and enforcement of patient rights span the public policy arena:

- a just-issued Medicare regulation establishing accelerated appeal rights for members denied care or ordered discharged from an inpatient facility
- a recent court case finding that HCFA has insufficiently enforced Medicare member appeal rights
- a legislative proposal to increase employee appeal rights under ERISA, including the right to sue the employer over medical policies
- provisions in proposed federal legislation allowing members to appeal coverage decisions to an outside party
- a recent court decision holding a health plan liable for its medical policies
- a requirement in the Balanced Budget Act (BBA) of 1997 instructing HCFA to distribute information on plan rules and appeal rights directly to Medicare beneficiaries

Consumer Empowerment

Health care policy makers believe their most powerful regulatory weapon is to unleash the marketwide phenomenon of the empowered consumer. Based on the theories of managed competition, the government would act as an information broker, providing consumers with comparative information on health plans and providers. The Medicare+Choice health information campaign is the federal government's first attempt in regulating the market as an information broker. The opportunity to educate and empower consumers is made possible by the convergence of several forces:

- the emergence of the Internet, which allows quick and effective transfer of information to consumers
- the development of health care performance measures and patient satisfaction instruments

- the increased demand for information brought on by the growth of managed care, the expanded range of health plan choices, and increased cost-sharing by the individual

MEDICARE+CHOICE APPLICATION PROCESS

A Medicare HMO application must be completed and the HMO reviewed by federal regulators before a Medicare HMO contract is awarded. The application process is twofold: the organization must start by filling out a core application similar to the current risk contract application, and then it must complete a supplemental application, to be available in June 1998, that incorporates provisions specific to the Medicare+Choice program. PSOs must start the process by going to their state regulatory agency to determine how the state intends to regulate PSOs. If a state's regulations exceed the Medicare+Choice requirements, particularly as they pertain to the solvency, then the PSO can apply to HCFA for a waiver. The state has 90 days to respond to the PSO's inquiry. The time frame from submission to approval of a Medicare+Choice application can last from six months to over one year.

A site visit by federal regulators is scheduled 10 to 15 weeks after the application is submitted (if the application is complete and the regulators do not have conflicting schedule problems). The site visit lasts three to five days. Generally, two persons from HCFA's central office and two from the regional office conduct the site visit. HCFA is organized into 10 regional offices. During the site visit, the leadership of the PSO should demonstrate a working knowledge of the Medicare+Choice program and should be prepared to answer any questions about their organization, the Medicare application, or the delivery system for the Medicare product. Actual notification of approval of the application, if all goes well, can be anticipated in 25 to 30 weeks, depending on the quality of the application and HCFA's backlog.

Premium Filings

Medicare+Choice plans must file an adjusted community rate (ACR) proposal in the Medicare risk contract application and annually thereafter. The ACR determines the maximum premium the Medicare+Choice plan can charge Medicare members. As part of the ACR proposal, the Medicare+Choice plan calculates the average payment rate (APR) anticipated from HCFA. The APR takes into account the anticipated demographic characteristics of the Medicare+Choice plan's membership. One APR is calculated for the entire service area covered by the Medicare contract. As a result, a county with a high adjusted average per capita cost (AAPCC) rate can subsidize a county with a lower rate if enrollment in both counties is equal.

MEDICARE+CHOICE REQUIREMENTS

Medicare+Choice plans are extensively regulated by HCFA, which promulgates rules and regulations governing the traditional fee-for-service Medicare system and the Medicare+Choice program. Medicare PSOs must meet federal guidelines in the following areas: financial solvency standards, provider contracting requirements, accessibility and availability, quality assurance programs, marketing activities, enrollment and disenrollment procedures, grievance and appeals procedures, and benefit offerings. If PSOs fail to meet the regulated qualifications set forth, the Department of Health and Human Services (DHHS) has authority to impose intermediate sanctions, including financial penalties, enrollment suspension, ceased payment, or contract termination.

Defining a PSO

The Balanced Budget Act of 1997 defines a PSO as a public or private entity established and operated by a provider or group of providers that directly supply a "substantial portion" of Medicare services. Providers are required to own 51 percent of for-profit Medicare PSOs or have 51 percent of the controlling membership of nonprofit PSOs. Regulations also require PSOs to provide 70 percent of Medicare services directly to beneficiaries

(60 percent of services in rural areas) or through affiliated providers. Affiliated providers are providers who have an ownership relationship with the PSO, are affiliated as a corporation, or share in the financial risk of the PSO. HCFA's interpretation of the BBA language allows PSOs that are very loosely structured. HCFA appears ready to interpret the definition of affiliated providers as meaning that providers need only accept some type of risk-sharing arrangement, such as a risk payment. HCFA could have affirmed a stricter interpretation and required the affiliated providers to have a risk in the ownership of the PSO, which would have drastically limited interest in PSO development. Instead providers may simply accept a risk-based payment as long as the payment exceeds a threshold set by HCFA.

Financial Solvency Standards

A negotiated rule making committee, in accordance with HCFA, devised PSO solvency standards. These standards will allow financially strong PSOs to operate while keeping weaker organizations out of the market. The final plan requires a PSO to have a net worth of $1.5 million, which may be decreased to no lower than $1 million with HCFA discretion. Of this net worth amount, $750,000 has to be held in cash. The PSO must fund its losses for the first 12 months of its financial plan. The result of the debate over intangible assets was a compromise; agreed to was a sliding scale that links the value of intangible assets that may be admitted to the amount of cash held toward meeting the net worth requirement. If the state solvency requirements are stricter than the federal standards, a PSO may apply to the federal government for a waiver of the state license requirements. The waiver is valid for three years, with the waiver program due to sunset in 2002.

Access and Scope of Coverage

PSOs must make services "available and accessible" to all subscribers "with reasonable promptness and whenever medically necessary." Medicare members must be able to reach a hospital and primary care physician within 30 minutes travel time or 30 miles of their home. Emergency services must be available 24 hours a day, seven days a week. Since a PSO must contract with a sufficient number of providers to ensure accessibility, it may have to add providers to its network area in order to receive HCFA's approval.

Even though a PSO may offer extra value-added benefits to its package, HCFA requires as a minimum the following services: physician services, hospital services, out-of-area emergency or urgent care services, laboratory and radiological tests, and preventive health services.

Provider Contracting

When a Medicare+Choice plan submits a Medicare contract application to DHHS, it must have a completed provider network in place. Before submitting an application, the plan must have all signed provider contracts that include specific Medicare-required language. The requirements cover a variety of regulatory and market issues distinctly related to the Medicare managed care product. See Exhibit 6–2 for a list of the major items.

Medicare+Choice plans must disclose information about physician incentive plans to HCFA. PSO compensation arrangements that place physicians or physician groups at substantial financial risk (as defined in the regulation) must provide adequate stop-loss protection and include the conducting of beneficiary surveys. PSOs must conduct a survey of its enrollees and recent disenrollees, to determine their level of satisfaction with the quality and access of care provided. The rule requires the survey be administered within one year after the date of an incentive arrangement and every two years afterwards.

Quality Assurance

A PSO must have an internal quality assurance program that is supervised by a quality assurance (QA) committee. HCFA requires the PSO to have in place systems to manage quality

Exhibit 6–2 Summary of Medicare Requirements for Provider Agreements

Legal
- Provide a hold harmless clause stating financial liability in case of insolvency
- Describe contract termination process
- Include provider agreement to maintain adequate liability and malpractice coverage
- Include clause making the provider contract nonassignable with PSO consent
- Include member nondiscrimination clause

Enrollment
- Identify who is eligible to enroll in the Medicare product
- State agreement to service the Medicare members
- Describe provider's responsibility for membership reporting

Payment
- Provide physician incentive payment protections, including stop-loss insurance (if required)
- Obligate provider to collect copayments and deductibles
- Obligate provider to handle coordination of benefit responsibilities
- Describe PSO's payment and administrative responsibilities

Services
- Comply with the Medicare+Choice peer review program
- Disclose advance directives to Medicare patients
- Disclose patient information to HCFA
- Explain Medicare appeals and grievance process
- Provide a detailed description of the PSO benefits
- Participate in the HMO's quality assurance activities, utilization management program, and member grievance system
- Grant physician admitting privileges in at least one contracting hospital
- Have physician provide notification of changes in licensure or admitting privileges
- Agree to provide services 24 hours a day, seven days a week
- Allow for PSO approval and oversight of subcontractor agreements

Courtesy of Ernst & Young LLP, Chicago, Illinois.

assurance and quality improvement in the provider network. The PSO must meet all of the HMO federal qualification requirements, which means that it must have a written QA plan, an internal quality peer review process, and a health outcomes focus; must perform individual physician and network pattern analysis; and must ensure that it receives physician feedback.

Marketing Activities

All marketing materials, including those developed for or by providers to market the plan, must be preapproved by HCFA. Additionally, all marketing materials must include detailed information on the benefits covered, coverage restrictions, and appeal process. A Medicare HMO evidence of coverage (EOC) or member handbook must be prepared for review. Generally, HMOs prepare two documents that explain HMO membership rules and benefits. The first is sent to beneficiaries before enrollment. It covers all of the important member issues required by HCFA but is very glossy and member-friendly. The second membership document is more legal in appearance and content and is analogous to an employer group subscriber agreement.

A PSO must present a marketing plan for its Medicare product when submitting its contract to HCFA. The marketing plan will describe the PSO's sales and marketing efforts; its staffing; its enrollment projections and a description of the market, including the size of the target market; and an evaluation of the competition. Increasingly, Medicare is focusing its fraud and abuse enforcement efforts on sales and marketing activities. PSOs should be concerned with developing oversight mechanisms to ensure that sicker, costlier beneficiaries are not discriminated against in marketing, sales, and member retention efforts.

Membership Accounting

The member enrollment process involves several steps, some of which are required by Medicare, others of which represent good customer service. There are different ways to process a member enrollment. HCFA recommends that health plans send letters informing the members of their proposed effective date of enrollment before HCFA confirmation and enrollment confirmation letters are sent (following the members' acceptance by HCFA). Also, a good way to build member allegiance and to reinforce member education is to follow up letters with phone calls. Some plans assign customer service representatives to members in an effort to better coordinate services and build allegiance by providing special treatment. After the members are enrolled, they are encouraged to attend an orientation session. At the orientation session, plan representatives go over membership rules with the new members. Also, a health evaluation and survey are completed for each member and forwarded to the member's primary care physician. New members who are at risk are called into the physician's office immediately for a health risk assessment.

The disenrollment process is similar to the enrollment process. Members are sent disenrollment letters before and after disenrollment is effective. Most importantly, a health plan should track disenrollment rates and the reasons members disenroll. The plan's management should implement and monitor benchmarks and should be concerned if the disenrollment rate is substantially higher than the national average or the competition. Disenrollment rates are affected by such factors as strength of the competition, similarity of benefits and premiums in the market, and the plan's performance.

Membership Systems

A Medicare managed care membership system is unique to the product. The membership processes respond to specific Medicare regulations and reporting requirements. Each month, plans submit member information to HCFA. The monthly membership transaction process allows HCFA to update its membership file for the plan, determine the enrollment totals, and process monthly capitation payments. In return, HCFA sends the plan summary reports on the membership transactions that were accepted or denied, a list of HCFA-initiated transactions, and other system maintenance actions. The plan's membership system and HCFA have no direct connection: the plan's system sends transactions, the HCFA system responds to those transactions, and vice versa. Twice a year, the plan can view what HCFA's membership file believes the plan's membership looks like. In the meantime, the health plan must use a series of reports to reconcile the two membership files and verify that they conform.

Data Submission

Health plans submit enrollment and payment information on every beneficiary in order to process the enrollment. To enroll in the health plan, a person must meet the eligibility criteria shown in Exhibit 6–3. Health plans can submit data using one of HCFA's data transfer systems, which involves implementing special software and maintaining the electronic link, or they can contract with a designated HCFA contractor.

Monthly Information Submission

The monthly information exchange begins by the health plan submitting its membership transactions, which are due to HCFA around the first week of the month. HCFA conducts an initial edit of the submitted transactions to verify that all necessary information is present and correctly entered. HCFA responds to each plan's submitted transaction with one of 67 potential

---

Exhibit 6–3 Minimum Eligibility Criteria

- Medicare Part B
- Resident in the service area
- Commercial age-ins outside of service area
- Do not have ESRD or Medicare hospice

Courtesy of Ernst & Young LLP, Chicago, Illinois.

responses. Of these potential responses, 10 are enrollment rejections related to eligibility issues. HCFA will soon provide all health plans with on-line eligibility verification, reducing the likelihood of enrollment rejections. A health plan benefits by immediately determining whether a prospective enrollee is eligible for Medicare, which saves time and money by eliminating rejections (which the health plan is required to manually investigate and resolve). The health plan is entitled to retroactive reimbursement for rejections that are due to HCFA errors but not its own, so it is in the health plan's best interest to ensure that information is accurate and complete before submitting it.

Demographic Tracking and Reporting

The health plan is responsible for tracking demographic information on its membership. HCFA places each member in a demographic category, also called a rate cell, for payment purposes. A member can be classified only under one rate cell. The order of priority for reporting the special classifications is as follows: ESRD, hospice, institutionalized, and Medicare-Medicaid. Below is a description of how health plans track and report demographic information.

Working Aged

Plans are required to assess and report the working status of current Medicare members annually and the working status of new members during enrollment. Current beneficiaries must be surveyed using a HCFA-approved questionnaire annually. However, Medicare+Choice plans are free to survey members more frequently and use additional methods to verify working status. Such methods may include direct-mail inquiries or information received directly from the employer.

Institutionalized Members

Medicare+Choice plans are required to verify and report members who reside in nursing homes. Accuracy is extremely important because monthly payments are increased by as much as 250 percent, depending on the member's age and sex. HCFA does not allow retroactive reimbursement for a plan's reporting error or omission. Unless otherwise notified monthly, HCFA will not list an enrollee as institutionalized. The beneficiary must reside in a qualified institutional facility at least 30 consecutive days in the prior month. A member's nursing home status can be detected through a variety of primary and secondary sources. However, primary verification should be used for reporting purposes. Primary verification can be achieved through monthly calls to nursing homes, a nursing home reporting system, or the plan's nursing home case management program.

Medicare-Medicaid

Payments for members who are Medicare-Medicaid dual eligible are also as high as 250 percent of the normal payment. States, through the "buy-in" program, report some of the dual eligibles to HCFA. Under the buy-in program, states pay the Medicare premium and potentially other member cost-sharing fees, such as deductibles and coinsurance, for low-income individuals called qualified Medicare beneficiaries (QMBs).

Medicare is concerned that health plans have an economic incentive to report dual eligibles and an economic incentive not to report when members lose dual-eligibility status. Once a member is on HCFA's membership file as being a dual eligible, the distinction remains until the plan or HCFA indicates otherwise. If a health plan tracks and reports dual eligibility, it must develop a system to reverify the member's eligibility status. Where possible, health plans are advised to negotiate the transfer of Medicare-Medicaid dual-eligible information from the state and use it as a primary data source for reporting to HCFA. Detection from secondary sources includes asking the member at initial enrollment, educating the members to notify the plan, issuing annual membership surveys, and identifying institutional members who are also Medicaid eligible. Verification and reverification should be from the primary source—the state Medicaid agency.

Hospital Encounter Data

Medicare+Choice plans will be required to submit hospital encounter data to HCFA for the development of a risk payment adjustor. The submission of "no-pay" bill data is mandated by Congress in an effort to implement a risk-adjusted payment system in 2000. The PSO must establish a mechanism to send the data to the local Medicare Part A carrier.

Claims Systems

The claims processing system must be reconfigured to meet Medicare's standards for timeliness, member notification, and provider payment limits. Claims originating within the plan's network are subject to the standards the plan negotiates with its contracting providers. Claims received outside the plan's network are subject to rules that apply to the Medicare fee-for-service system. Medicare+Choice plans must pay claims from noncontracting providers at the Medicare payment levels and within specific time periods. HCFA regulators review the plan's claim processing system during their site visit review. See Exhibit 6–4 for a description of the regulatory requirements.

Appeals and Grievances

Medicare has a different process for handling member complaints, referred to as grievances and appeals. In the commercial health plan market, all member complaints are classified together. Medicare requires health plans to classify and process appeals and grievances separately. Disputes about the health plan's or a provider's determination to provide or pay for a service are resolved through the Medicare appeals procedures. Complaints about member satisfaction, quality, or other issues not related to a service or coverage denial are treated through the appeals process.

Exhibit 6–4 Medicare Claims Processing Requirements

- Clean claims are processed within 30 days.
- All claims are processed within 60 days.
- All member notices, including explanation of benefits, are approved by HCFA.
- Out-of-network claims for hospital, physicians, renal dialysis, and skilled nursing facility services are paid according to Medicare payment limits.
- Member cost sharing is calculated correctly.
- Interest is paid on claims exceeding the processing time frames.
- Contracting providers who process claims meet the Medicare requirement.

Courtesy of Ernst & Young LLP, Chicago, Illinois.

All Medicare appeals must be processed within 60 days. However, a member may request an expedited review if the standard time frame jeopardizes the life or health of the enrollee or the enrollee's ability to regain maximum function. In the case of an expedited review, written confirmation must be mailed to the enrollee within two working days. Appeals must be signed by the member but can be received over the telephone and written down by a customer service representative. Members do not have to file appeals with the plan, and on rare occasions members file appeals with the Social Security Office or Railroad Retirement Board.

Member Education

Much policy and public debate has been focused on health plans' processing of Medicare member appeals. Critics claim health plans do a poor job of educating members on their appeal rights and the appeals process. As part of the determination notice, the health plan or provider must include a description of the member's appeal rights. HCFA reviews claims and appeals correspondence to ensure that proper information is communicated to members. In response to the public scrutiny of the

Table 6–1 Medicare+Choice Regulatory Requirements and Leading Practices

Key Operational Business Processes	*Example of Regulatory Requirement*	*Example of Leading Practice*
Marketing		
Market research Product development Marketing materials Member communication Sales, advertising, public relations Regulatory monitoring	Marketing materials submitted for prior review and approval	Performance measurement by product lines and market segments
Network development		
Credentialing Practice profiling Contract negotiations Provider administrative procedures Network adequacy Provider servicing	Substantial portion of services provided in-network Medicare-certified providers Availability and accessibility standards	Provide profiling determines network participation decisions
Claims		
Other party liability Coordination of benefit recoveries Electronic claim submissions Claims adjudication protocols Multiple product adjudication capability (HMO, POS, FFS) Productivity quality guidelines Coordination with utilization management	Medicare claims processing software Specific definitions and standards	Electronic claims submission by physicians and hospitals
Health service delivery and utilization management		
Treatment protocols Practice guidelines Quality improvement program Continuum of care coordination Risk-sharing arrangements	Written QA plan Internal quality peer review process Health outcomes focus	Disease management and practice guidelines to control utilization levels

continues

Table 6–1 continued

Key Operational Business Processes	*Example of Regulatory Requirement*	*Example of Leading Practice*
Utilization monitoring by type of service UM linked to network development and benefit design	Individual physician and network pattern analysis Physician feedback	
Finance/actuarial services		
Reinsurance arrangements Medical/administrative loss ratio analysis Revenue, enrollment, and utilization projections Reserve calculations Regulatory and other capital requirements	Adjusted community rating Solvency protection requirements	Capital reserves tied to premium revenues
Management information systems		
Member level data capability Multiple product capability Utilization management modules Provider profiling Health Plan Employer Data and Information Set (HEDIS) reporting capability	Systematic data collection of quality and utilization management indicators Routine and ad hoc reporting capabilities	Electronic adjudication of claims and authorizations
Member services and enrollment		
Grievance and appeals procedures Enrollment reconciliation Inquiry monitoring and analysis Member outreach programs Member satisfaction surveys	Member satisfaction surveys A Medicare enrollment and disenrollment system A Medicare appeals system	Member satisfaction survey–driven operational improvements

Courtesy of Ernst & Young LLP, Chicago, Illinois

appeals process, health plans should review their current efforts to educate members on the appeals process.

CONCLUSION

Simply meeting regulatory requirements is not sufficient in the competitive Medicare market; to attract and retain members, organizations will need to be high performers in every business process. See Table 6–1 for a description of the potential regulatory requirements and leading business practices for each area. Public policy will increasingly be a driver of consumerism in health care, making it imperative for Medicare+Choice plans to be more consumer focused and to compete by providing greater value to Medicare beneficiaries. The regulatory process should be taken seriously, not only to avoid regulatory troubles but also to recognize trends in an important market driver.

CHAPTER 7

Information Technology Requirements of Provider Sponsored Organizations

Scott Kolesar, Dave Vreeland, and Kimberly Zinman

Health care information systems currently perform the tasks for which they are programmed. Like systems in other industries, they reflect and reinforce the operating structures within which they function. For health care information technology (IT) to support a provider sponsored organization (PSO) requires a shared vision of the organization, its scope, and its mission. Successful definition requires management to take a functional process oriented view of the organization, a view that crosses departmental boundaries. It requires that management objectively assess the organization's capabilities to move from a provider-focus solution to a combined provider-payer information technology solution.

The questions addressed in this chapter include the following:

- How to migrate an organization from a provider-only technology solution to one that can support payer requirements?
- What are PSO information requirements?
- What application software is required to support a PSO?
- How should PSO management address buy versus outsource decisions when it comes to application software?
- What are the IT organization and infrastructure requirements?

- What is the state of the managed care application vendor market?

This chapter describes the most important steps PSO executives can take to ensure that their information infrastructure supports their business strategy.

HEALTH CARE INFORMATION TECHNOLOGY STRATEGIES IN TRANSITION

Much has been written in this age of information technology about the degree to which the health care industry has traditionally lagged behind other industries in terms of the investment in information systems and services. Health care's level of commitment to information systems—only 2–3 percent of operating expenses versus 6–8 percent in manufacturing and 8–12 percent in banking[1]—is ironic given the widespread belief that better information is the key to controlling costs and improving the quality of care.

Yet, this clearly is beginning to change owing to the need to provide better clinical decision support and managed care's replacement of traditional indemnity (or fee-for-service) payment mechanisms throughout the country, which has created an environment that is arguably much more information intensive than industries such as banking. A further driver of change is the rise of integrated delivery and financing systems (IDFSs), organizations that theoretically provide all aspects of care delivery and financing, essentially serving as payer and provider. Another type of organization that will see a blending of payer and provider characteristics is the PSO.

In the case of both types of organization, the challenges facing them result from their attempting to enter what is essentially a different line of business utilizing the human resources, operational and marketing capabilities, and IT capabilities of their previous business specialties. In the case of PSOs (and to a certain extent IDFSs), an additional challenge will be to transform the organization from provider to provider-payer and then to Medicare payer (see Figure 7–1). This is the key challenge in many ways facing organizations interested in entering the PSO market, particularly from the perspective of IT requirements.

INFORMATION TECHNOLOGY STANDARDS FOR HOSPITAL AND PHYSICIAN ORGANIZATIONS

Provider Organizational Arrangements

Historically there have been various arrangements in the marketplace to bring physicians together and to bring hospitals and physicians together. These include the following:

- physician organizations (POs)
- independent practitioner associations (IPAs)
- group practices without walls
- physician hospital organizations (PHOs)
- management service organizations (MSOs)
- foundation models
- integrated salaried models

These organizations have developed in response to changing health care financing mechanisms that find payment for health

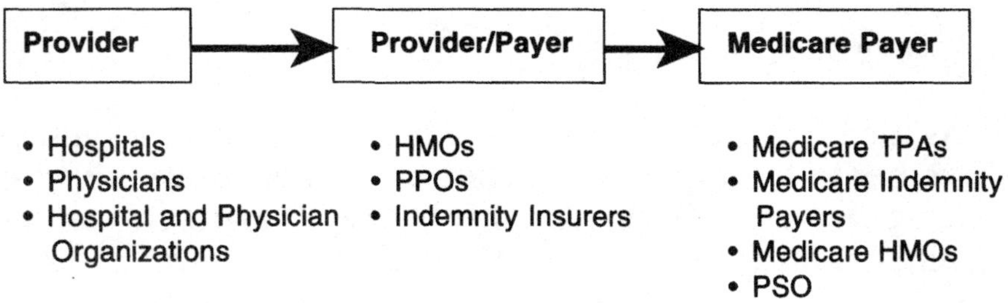

Figure 7–1 PSO: The transitional challenge for providers. Courtesy of Ernst & Young LLP, Chicago, Illinois.

care services moving from being indemnity or fee-for-service based to being managed care based. Thus, hospital CEOs give three main reasons for their development and existence: (1) to protect hospital markets, (2) to expand health system markets, and (3) to integrate and coordinate care delivery.[2]

Traditional Provider Information Technology Functionality

Figure 7–2 describes the functional IT transition that must take place in order for provider organizations to have the types of IT capabilities needed to support a PSO. "Previously operating as independent business entities, the hospitals, physician practices, and other organizations that form today's IDS initially focused on automating financial and administrative functions."[3] Thus traditional provider IT functionality has included automated

- patient scheduling
- registration
- charge entry
- coding
- claims and statement production
- accounts receivable management
- collections
- general accounting

As the integrated forms of these heretofore disparate entities have begun to develop in reaction to a marketplace driven by managed care, the IT functionality has begun to develop as well, giving provider organizations the ability to manage the financial risk associated with some types of managed care.

In the current health care environment, provider organizations are called upon to manage a variety of health insurance contract types with varying degrees of risk. In order to do this, IT

Provider

- Patient scheduling
- Registration
- Charge entry
- Coding
- Claims/statement production
- Accounts receivable management
- Collections
- General accounting

Provider/Payer

- Core systems
  - –Benefit administration
  - –Claims adjudication and payment
  - –Group (account) administration
  - –IBNR analysis
  - –Capitation management
  - –Contract management
  - –Premium billing
  - –Reinsurance/stop-loss insurance
  - –Accounts payable/accounts receivable/general ledger
- Marketing and sales
  - –Prospective tracking
  - –Market research
  - –Broker sales commission marketing
  - –Employer reporting
- Patient/customer management
  - –Membership/enrollment marketing
  - –Customer service
- Network/provider management
  - –Provider credentialing
  - –Provider profiling
  - –PCP panel assignment
  - –Capitation/risk pools
- Utilization management
  - –Concurrent review and case management
  - –Referrals and authorizations management
  - –Demand management
  - –Pharmacy benefit management

Medicare Payer

- All standard provider/payer functionality plus
  - –Medicare enrollment management
  - –Medicare claims processing
  - –Medicare ECP/EFT
  - –Medicare quality reporting
  - –HEDIS reporting

Figure 7–2 PSO information systems functionality transition. Courtesy of Ernst & Young LLP, Chicago, Illinois.

functionality must go beyond billing and collections and the automation of administrative tasks and provide organizations with the ability to manage multiple payer contracts effectively. This is because the driving force in a managed care environment is cost reduction as well as improvement of the quality of care. Thus, in addition to the traditional functionality listed above, the following automated functions, some of which are provider/payer functions (see Figure 7–2), have begun to make their way onto the forefront of health care IT:

- *core systems*—benefit administration (covered/not covered services), contract management, accounts payable/accounts receivable/general ledger
- *patient/customer management*—eligibility verification, customer service, electronic medical record (EMR), enterprisewide registration/master member index
- *network management/provider file maintenance*—provider profiling, primary care provider panel assignment
- *utilization management*—concurrent review and case management, referrals and authorizations management

The various provider organizational arrangements that exist in the marketplace today have begun to utilize the above automated managed care support systems in a variety of ways and to varying degrees.

THE INFORMATION TECHNOLOGY REQUIREMENTS OF A RISK-BEARING ENTITY (PAYER)

Despite the enhanced functionality of today's provider-based managed care support systems, there is evidence that these systems are not capable of supporting a payer's business needs when the core business functions are those of a payer and not a provider. The systems and functionality required to support a payer are more sophisticated than the provider-based systems offering managed care functionality; they are listed in detail in Figure 7–2.

As discussed, in order for an organization to make the transition from provider to PSO, an intermediate step is necessary: becoming a risk-bearing organization or payer. What is meant by this is not the process of accepting capitation from an insurance company and managing a defined population of patients, but rather the process of contracting directly with a governmental entity or employer to provide all necessary health care services to a group of employees or beneficiaries, thereby eliminating the "third party" and combining the payer and provider functions within one organization.

To achieve this initial step toward becoming a PSO, a provider organization must shore up a number of resources and raise the level of competency among its teams. In addition, besides addressing human resources, marketing, and general operating functions, it must obtain the appropriate IT infrastructure.

"The capital requirements to start up an HMO are significant, and many provider sponsored plans will find themselves competing against large publicly traded HMOs with ready access to capital."[4] The initial capital requirements range from $2 million to $10 million, and IT expenses account for a substantial portion of the total amount. Organizations truly interested in entering the payer business must treat IT issues very seriously. Identifying the information requirements and system functionality is a critical first step in defining the IT needs of the new business. Embarking upon a formal system selection process to determine the most appropriate vendor given the identified functional and business needs is the recommended next step.

A consideration that often arises is whether adding functionality to the provider's existing IT arrangement is sufficient to support the business needs of a risk-bearing entity. As described above, the functionality required to effectively manage the care of a defined population of patients is significant. While many vendors in the hospital and physician practice management system business have begun to offer effective integrated solutions, it is generally believed that the system needs are too large to be met by current provider-based systems.[5]

A further consideration is the level of expertise of the personnel who will support and operate the information system. This issue highlights the importance of experience in the payer business. Suffice it to say that the IT department of a provider organization may not have the experience required to appropriately support the implementation and operation of the payer system.

APPLICATION SOFTWARE REQUIREMENTS OF A PSO

Even with the most sophisticated payer-based systems, newly developing PSOs will be challenged to meet the Health Care Financing Administration (HCFA) requirements to enter the Medicare market. According to the *Medicare Health Maintenance Organization/Competitive Medical Plan Manual,* which outlines operational standards for entities contracting with HCFA, an organization must have "sufficient administrative support, reporting and recordkeeping capacity, to meet Medicare requirements effectively and efficiently."[6] These tasks will be even more demanding for organizations without the technical or operational expertise necessary to perform at the expected level set by HCFA.

The greatest administrative demand for PSOs will be in the arena of patient (customer) management systems. Membership management will take on a whole new meaning as PSOs are faced with the necessity of collecting, tracking, and submitting eligibility and membership data on a continuous basis. In addition to meeting the current contracted payer requirements, PSOs will need to develop infrastructure and systems to meet the new quality requirements. HCFA has specified that Health Employer Data and Information Set 3.0 (HEDIS) will be the standard against which PSOs will be measured. Maintaining this complex and robust set of measures will require system, application, and resource expenditures. Bruce Fried, formerly the Director for Health Plans and Providers at HCFA, stated, "Dealing with HCFA and managing the Medicare population at full risk is more challenging than hospitals are anticipating. Information system requirements and the investment will be enormous, particularly as we start to demand performance data."[7]

Membership Accounting

Membership management becomes a fundamental competency for risk-bearing organizations as they transform themselves from provider-payers into Medicare provider-payers. Membership accounting is the most important operational function that a PSO will undertake, and its ability to manage membership information will be crucial to its financial success in a risk arrangement with HCFA.

Demographic and health status data elements that need to be collected during Medicare enrollment and tracked on an ongoing basis include

- working status
- institutionalized status
- Medicaid eligibility
- hospice care
- diagnosis of end-stage renal disease (ESRD)

These data elements are specific to the determination of Medicare coverage and directly impact a Medicare member's eligibility and the premium payment made to the PSO. The PSO must capture these data elements up front and monitor them for changes on an ongoing basis. The importance of membership tracking can be explained by using an example of institutionalized status. Medicare will reimburse current health plans holding a risk contract with HCFA "as much as 250 percent"[8] above the average monthly reimbursement rate for members who have been a resident for 30 days or longer in an institutional facility. Without the necessary resources and technology for tracking member stays in nursing facilities, an organization may not be aware of a member's inpatient status and will end up incurring costs for care without receiving appropriate reimbursement.

In addition to collecting and monitoring key demographic and health status indicators, the PSO must verify the accuracy of the collected data prior to submission. Once the enrollment information is collected and verified by the PSO, it is submitted to HCFA for beneficiary validation with HCFA's Group Health Plan Master Record System (GHP Master). HCFA will respond with a listing of accepted and rejected membership records. The PSO will not only be denied payment for rejected membership records but will most likely be responsible for investigating and reporting to HCFA on the rejected membership records. Retroactive enrollment and reimbursement would be allowed for rejections due to HCFA errors but not for errors on the part of the PSO.

The challenge of obtaining accurate enrollment information does not end once the member is effectively enrolled in an organization. Medicare members can disenroll and reenroll under the Medicare+Choice Program on a monthly basis. Other reasons for disenrollment include termination of Medicare entitlement, permanent departure from the geographic area, or disenrollment for cause, to name a few. Given all the possible scenarios for terminating enrollment, it is not uncommon for payer organizations to have difficulty managing their membership.

The task of membership management will be made easier in the near future when HCFA provides on-line eligibility verification. For now, Medicare risk organizations cannot interface with HCFA's GHP Master system to validate eligibility information and are left to reconcile manually HCFA membership reports with their own membership system. Although on-line membership validation has yet to be implemented, payers can submit enrollment information electronically by purchasing and maintaining a HCFA data transfer system or contracting with a designated HCFA contractor.[9]

Claims Processing

Performing claims processing also entails meeting stringent HCFA requirements, which can mean reconfiguring even the most sophisticated payer-based system. Medicare claims processing requirements are as follows:[10]

- Clean claims are processed within 30 days.
- All claims are processed within 60 days.
- All member notices, including the explanation of benefits, are approved by HCFA.
- Out-of-network claims for hospital, physician, renal dialysis, and skilled nursing facility services are paid according to Medicare payment limits.
- Member cost sharing is calculated correctly.
- Interest is paid on claims exceeding the processing time frames.
- Contracting providers who process claims meet the standard Medicare requirements.

Due to specific HCFA enrollment and claims requirements, payers traditionally have set up their Medicare product as a distinct business unit, separate from their commercial plan.[11] Payers can then educate their staff in the Medicare unit on the operational policies and procedures and technology that are needed to run a Medicare product line effectively.

The Appeals and Grievances Tracking System

Medicare requires that all appeals are processed within 60 days and reported to HCFA. In order to comply with the processing time frame, organizations will need to devise an efficient process for tracking and routing grievances to various departments within an organization. Whether this function needs to be automated will depend on the volume of Medicare members. HCFA uses the Beneficiary Tracking System to monitor grievances that have been filed with contracted organizations.

Quality Assurance

Currently, the HMO/CMP manual requires that organizations monitor the adequacy of their provider networks and the ability of Medicare members to obtain health services. The manual only goes as far as stating that organizations must "have systems in place to collect health services data to evaluate the availability and accessibility of services."[12] Most of the required data can be collected over the phone and will likely be captured by the customer service department. Other required information can be gathered by surveying physician practices or through the back-end processing of claims. Various desktop applications have the ability to track current measures and allow organizations to perform the necessary analysis. With the advent of HEDIS 3.0 as the standard set of quality performance measures for contracted organizations, PSOs will need to assess the ability of systems to generate the necessary indicators. The National Committee for Quality Assurance (NCQA) has released *HEDIS 3.0 Volume 2: Technical Specifications* to prepare organizations for the various system requirements needed to implement HEDIS effectively.[13]

HEDIS Requirements

HEDIS, an ever-evolving set of data reporting standards, is designed to provide some standardization in performance reporting for financial, utilization, membership, and clinical data so that employers and others can compare performance among plans. The collection, storage, and dissemination of HEDIS data is critical to gaining NCQA accreditation. Recommended actions that can be taken up-front are as follows:

- Collect data for all services rendered for your patient population, including all ancillaries providers who may be contracted rather than affiliated providers. Required HEDIS data elements are listed in detail in Exhibit 7–1.
- Require the submission of encounter data.
- Set up links to a centralized data repository for all contracted providers so that claims and enrollment data can be shared.
- Set up performance contracts with providers that reward data submission.

Exhibit 7–1 Data Elements Required for Performance Measurement by Domain

Effectiveness of care

1. Demographics
   - Age
   - Sex
   - Education
   - Employment
   - Income
   - Race
   - Ethnicity
   - Language
   - Marital status
2. Insurance information
   - Insurance type
   - Product types (e.g., HMO, PPO, POS)
   - Medicaid, Medicare, commercial
   - Specific benefits (e.g., pharmacy, prenatal)
   - Enrollment periods, start of enrollment, breaks in enrollment
   - Health plan identifier
3. Provider information
   - Identifier
   - Specialties
   - Certifications
   - Languages
4. Health-related risk behaviors
   - Tobacco use
   - Exercise
   - Diet
   - Nonprescribed drugs
   - Sexual activity
5. Clinical
   - Signs and symptoms
   - Preventative services
   - Performance of diagnostic procedures, evaluations, tests
   - Diagnoses
   - Performance of treatment services
   - Treatments delivered
   - Dates of treatment

continues

Exhibit 7–1 continued

- Referrals and consultations
- Guideline compliance rates

6. Health-related functional assessments, and outcomes of assessments
7. Service events
   - Emergency department visits
   - Outpatient visits
   - Inpatient hospital stays
   - Visits to mental health institutions
   - Service time, duration, date

Access/availability of care

1. Availability of a service
   - On site and by contract
2. Capacity to provide services at an appropriate level (e.g., specialized evaluations and treatment)
3. Waiting times
   - Appointments (by time appointment made, time appointment kept, urgency)
   - Time needed to access emergency services
4. Distance and travel time between facilities for referral services
5. After-hours provider coverage
6. Language concordance between providers and patients

Satisfaction with the experience of care

1. Provider and patient experiences and preferences and elicited perceptions, thoughts, and feelings
2. Directives
3. Consents
4. Patient satisfaction with the experience of care
5. Patient reports on care episodes
6. Provider satisfaction

Informed health care choices

1. Health plan patient education
   - General education activities
   - Health education and information presented to patients with specified indications
2. Patient knowledge about health care decisions

Source: National Committee for Quality Assurance. *A Roadmap for Information Systems, Evolving Systems to Support Performance Measurement,* HEDIS 3.0/1998, Volume 4.

- Ensure the accuracy of data. NCQA suggests that "entry of data into the system should, to the greatest extent possible, be done by the person responsible for collecting the information."
- Use industry standards.
- Use "unique enrollee identifiers" so that members can be tracked across servicing providers and over the course of time. This is especially important for Medicare members who can disenroll and reenroll on a monthly basis.
- Stay away from the use of "home-grown" codes or be able to map these codes to standard codes.
- Establish and ensure the security and confidentiality of member information. This will become more important as greater amounts of clinical information become managed by information systems.

Premium Collection, Accounts Receivable, and Disbursement

HCFA is set up to perform electronic funds transfer through the automatic clearinghouse and strongly encourages contracted organizations to use this mechanism for payment. Once the premium payment is made to the organization, the PSO will need to allocate and disburse appropriate payments to various health care providers. Crucial to this function is the ability to tie the premium to the various payment arrangements that have been negotiated with network providers. Obviously, the more complicated the payment arrangements, the more sophisticated the technology needs to be.

STATE OF THE MANAGED CARE VENDOR MARKET

One of the critical questions regarding today's managed care application vendor market is, which managed care application vendors and service providers will succeed? Currently, while the demand for managed care applications is increasing, the supply of viable vendor options is decreasing due to product obsolescence and industry consolidation.[14] In fact, the managed care application vendor market is dominated by a few large vendor organizations, and the other vendors in the market are in a state of transition. They either are focusing on the development of new managed care products in anticipation of growth or they are facing an ever-decreasing market share due to an inability to meet market needs.

GETTING THERE: MEETING THE INFORMATION TECHNOLOGY REQUIREMENTS

As has been highlighted throughout this chapter, capital, implementation time, system training, and experienced personnel are critical factors to consider when deciding how to provide the information and the system functionality needed to operate a PSO effectively. Once the operational needs and requirements have been identified, the PSO is ready to determine the most beneficial way to provide the necessary functionality. The PSO should spend a significant amount of time researching and evaluating not only payer systems but companies that outsource systems and staff. The critical factors above should serve as measures for the PSO in the evaluation process.

The information technology options for PSOs to evaluate are to

- purchase an integrated provider/payer information system
- purchase additional payer-based functionality to be integrated with the existing provider system
- utilize a service bureau arrangement
- outsource the system and staff

Purchasing an Integrated Provider-Payer System

Most PSOs that go through the evaluation process in order to select an integrated provider-payer system will determine that it is not practical or economical to purchase and implement an integrated provider-payer system when the volume of business is uncertain and the cost to build and maintain the required technology and IT organization infrastructure is substantial. In order to justify the purchase of an integrated provider/payer information system, a PSO would need to have between 75,000 and 100,000 members to reach the break-even point (the point where annual outsourcing transaction costs begin to exceed the cost of acquiring and maintaining an in-house system on a yearly basis).

Purchasing Additional Payer-Based Functionality To Be Integrated with the Existing Provider System

A PSO just entering managed care, with relatively few contracts and a small provider network, may be able to get by with the managed care module of its practice management software suite. Once a PSO begins to negotiate with many payers that offer complex benefit plans (e.g., point-of-service and triple option plans) and to participate in extensive and overlapping provider networks, a core claims and administrative system is required. The Gartner Group reports that managed care modules developed by practice management system vendors will not be fully functional until the year 2000. Until then, PSOs are advised to also evaluate core claims and administrative systems that support complex claims processing. Scenarios used during demonstrations are the best way to identify which vendor package can support the PSO's claims processing requirements. At a minimum, the practice management managed care module must support the

- enrollment and disenrollment of members
- changing of benefit plans, primary care providers, and member numbers
- addition and updating of benefit plans
- addition and editing of providers (hospitals, physicians, clinicians) and provider groups

- addition, updating, and termination of fee schedules
- linking of providers and others to fee schedules
- addition and edition of referrals
- linking of referrals to appointments in patient scheduling
- linking of referrals to encounters and claims
- closing of referrals
- entering of claims
- editing of claims
- generation of claims payment
- reversing of paid claims
- running of reports (financial, medical management, utilization and quality management)

Utilizing a Service Bureau or Information Technology Outsourcing Vendor

The limited and somewhat costly options described previously leaves PSO management to consider either a service bureau outsourcing arrangement or an IT outsourcing arrangement. Service bureau outsourcing is the outsourcing of one or more key business processes, generally claims, enrollment, referral management, customer service, or management reporting of the realted IT infrastructure. IT outsourcing is a contractual relationship between the PSO and an external and generally unrelated vendor, with the vendor assuming responsibility for one or more IT functions. This generally involves transfer of assets to the external vendor, including hardware, software, facilities, and personnel. In rare circumstances, IT outsourcing may also include support for one or more business functions.[15]

The pros of a service bureau or outsourcing arrangement are that it

- limits the initial capital requirements for software and hardware and thus increases the operating capital requirements

- decreases the infrastructure costs required to support the required IT organization
- reduces time to solution and implementation costs
- minimizes PSO staffing commitments and expenses
- allows the PSO to focus on its core competencies

Since the IT and administrative services required to administer at-risk managed care business are frequently beyond a PSO's financial or business scope, outsourcing will be a dominant strategy.

The items to consider when selecting an outsourcing or service bureau vendor include

- contract terms and conditions
- managed care experience
- Medicare experience
- client base and client satisfaction
- financial stability of the vendor
- vendor's vision or strategy
- cultural alignment
- geographic location
- capacity for future growth
- competition

Although outsourcing seems to be the appropriate IT solution for most PSOs, there are certain general functions that a PSO should never outsource because of their business impact and HCFA regulations. These functions are medical management, appeals and grievances, and to a lesser extent customer service. They have in common the need for critical decision making and high levels of communication. This is not to say that separate systems or applications need to be purchased. Rather a PSO could contract with one vendor under a service bureau arrangement for a complete payer-based system and have certain functional areas such as claims processing and membership management performed by the vendor's staff while the critical functional areas would be operated by the PSO's internal staff. Maintenance of the entire system would still remain the responsibility of the vendor.

A PSO also can take an incremental approach to IT development, by outsourcing to a vendor whose system can eventually be brought in-house. This approach allows the PSO to gain a good sense of what the membership volume will be and what system resources and staffing experts will be needed to maintain the system. It also allows the current staff to gradually learn the system from the vendor experts who are handling their specific account.

INFORMATION TECHNOLOGY CHALLENGES FOR PROVIDERS WISHING TO ENTER THE PSO MARKET

This final section serves as an overview of the key IT issues provider organizations face in attempting to enter the PSO market.

Capital

As discussed, a significant portion of the PSO start-up costs are related to the acquisition of the information system, staffing, and technology infrastructure needed to support the business. Providers with an operational commercial HMO (i.e., provider-payers) have the advantage that a system is (hopefully) already in place. However, the additional requirements of a PSO (i.e., a "Medicare" HMO) may present a hurdle that requires upgrading or even replacement of the existing system.

Integration

It has been pointed out that the current managed care functionality of most provider-based systems is not sufficient to support an HMO operation. The upshot is that the system that an organization ultimately selects to support its payer functions must be integrated with the provider-based systems to enhance the seamless delivery of care to the members. Moreover, because of the PSO requirements of said systems, it is even more critical to ensure that the selected application can provide electronic exchange of data with HCFA. Given the lack of standardization of benefits data among systems, the integration issue can be a major barrier to success.

Core Competencies

The business of providing health care insurance services is very different from that of providing health care services. The current state of provider-based systems does not support a payer's business needs because the core business competencies are fundamentally different. As the marketplace continues to evolve and the lines dividing providers and payers blur, perhaps the health care system vendors will begin to develop applications that support these businesses more effectively; however, today these core system competencies remain somewhat distinct.

Operational Experience and Technical Competencies

Just as the system functionality differs between providers and payers, so does the experiential backgrounds of the individuals operating and supporting the systems. It is therefore critically important that the IT department makes a concerted effort to staff the implementation and ultimately the system support departments with individuals who have experience with managed care systems, preferably in an environment supporting Medicare managed care. Bridging the gap between provider and payer and between payer and Medicare payer is one of the biggest challenges from an overall and an IT perspective.

HCFA Requirements

The requirements placed on an organization by HCFA are not insignificant and must be considered from an IT perspective. Failure to meet the reporting requirements of HCFA, despite the organization's ability to manage the cost and quality of care in the PSO, can result in severe penalties and loss of premium revenue. To ensure that this potential pitfall does not hinder the success of the PSO, the organization must understand the various HCFA operating and reporting requirements, ensure that the IT functionality can support such requirements, and hire sufficiently experienced personnel to utilize the systems to the PSO's best advantage.

CONCLUSION

The next few years will be a time of transition and turbulence for PSO executives and IT practitioners. A growing PSO market is demanding more sophisticated practice management information systems that address the needs of larger group practices managing risk contracts. Provider-based PSOs looking to replace or upgrade their practice management systems must also evaluate their managed care options. Vendors, responding to this market expansion opportunity, are developing provider-payer automation suites that offer traditional practice management and managed care functionality. An increasing number of managed care IT vendors and managed care organizations will be offering service bureau and IT outsourcing services to the PSO market.

As the PSO market grows, consolidates, and matures, PSO IT options will rapidly expand. Each of the alternatives will need to be evaluated in terms of its alignment with the business strategy of the organization. After all, the ability of a PSO to thrive and compete successfully in a highly competitive marketplace lies in its ability to deploy and maintain systems to manage mission-critical information.

Providers should develop a mental checklist of important items for deploying technology to meet the needs of a PSO. The following questions need careful consideration by health care organizations in general and those with an interest in entering the PSO marketplace:

- Has an IT plan been developed?
- Does senior management understand and support it?
- Does the plan support the PSO's business strategy?
- Is it realistic? Has it been objectively critiqued?
- Is the PSO capable of implementing it?
- Do IT personnel (if any) have the proper skills?
- Do PSO users understand their roles and responsibilities?
- Is there a structured, disciplined approach to implementation?
- Are resources committed and are expectations realistic?

If these questions can be answered in the affirmative, there is a good chance that the implementation of an IT solution for the organization will achieve a measurable degree of success. A thoughtfully contrived IT plan that aligns with the business strategy of the PSO can serve as a guide to support both near- and long-term decision making as it relates to managing information systems.

NOTES

1. T. Reynolds, "Informatting the IDS," *HIMSS News* 6 (1995).
2. J. A. Alexander, "An Exploratory Analysis of Market-based, Physician-Organization Arrangements," *Hospital and Health Services Administration 41,* no. 3 (1996): 311–329.
3. D. Richmond, "Information Systems for Integrated Delivery Systems: Putting the Pieces Together," *Healthcare Executive and Management Strategies,* 19 December, 1996, 7–9.

4. F.M. Prescott and B. Carlson, "What Providers Need To Know about Starting up an HMO," *Medical Network Strategy Report* 5, no. 11 (1996): 7–9.

5. J. Carr, "Can Provider-based Systems Support Payers?" *Managed Care Applications and Vendors* (Gartner Group Research Note), 27 February, 1997.

6. *Medicare Health Maintenance Organization/Competitive Medical Plan Manual,* HCFA Pub. 75.

7. Ernst and Young, *Mapping Your Competitive Position* (Chicago: 1997).

8. Ernst and Young, *The Winds of Change: A Guide to Medicare Managed Care* (Chicago: 1996).

9. Ibid.

10. Ibid.

11. Ernst and Young, *The Winds of Change.*

12. *Medicare Health Maintenance Organization/Competitive Medical Plan Manual,* HCFA Pub. 75.

13. National Committee for Quality Assurance. *A Roadmap for Information Systems, Evolving Systems to Support Performance Measurement,* HEDIS 3.0/1998, Volume 4. HEDIS®is a registered trademark of the National Committee for Quality Assurance.

14. J. Carr, "Managed Care Application Market Shakes Out," *Managed Care Applications and Vendors,* (Gartner Group Research Note), 21 November, 1997.

15. J. Young, "Outsourcing Interest Among HMOs Wanes," *Managed Care Applications and Vendors,* (Gartner Group Research Note), 30 October, 1997.

CHAPTER 8

Shared or Delegated Services with Provider Owners

Colleen E. Dowd and William Anderson

Providers can share many administrative functions with health plans. In fact, it is to their advantage to assume responsibility for many of these services to increase their control in the delivery of care and to collect and manage the data that these functions generate. This sharing of services is supported by a formal and detailed delegation agreement, which transfers the performance of but not the responsibility for these functions.

Regardless of a senior health plan's sponsorship, there are certain challenges that must be overcome. For instance, enrollees expect managed care plans to deliver higher quality care at a lower cost than traditional Medicare. They also want increased access to wellness and preventative programs.

However, as the senior population ages and faces more complex chronic conditions, enrollees also expect health plans to maintain a high level of service and care, regardless of the clinical complications (and financial burdens) that are involved with taking care of older and sicker patients. Perhaps the greatest challenge lies in a health plan's ability to demonstrate, through established monitoring systems, the highest clinical outcomes and the most efficient use of resources.

Providers that sponsor PSOs are faced with establishing and maintaining a dual relationship with seniors. Their first role is as traditional caregivers. Their second is as owners or sponsors of the provider sponsored organization (PSO). Unfortunately, the incentives for each relationship are not always aligned. In fact, in some cases they are diametrically opposed. Using risk contracting, providers are more likely to align financial incentives, which should lead to higher aligned clinical incentives and improved administrative coordination. It is this sharing of financial risk that is the basis for PSOs.

Although there are many challenges for providers that operate PSOs, there are also significant opportunities. Since providers have to "wear two hats," they are in a position to consolidate functions and thereby create efficiencies while improving the administration of both their provider and PSO operations.

Providers can share administrative functions with a PSO. PSOs may also delegate health plan functions to a provider entity. Functions that may be shared or delegated include claims payment, credentialing, utilization management, quality improvement, member relations, and medical records.

WHAT IS DELEGATION?

With delegation, the PSO authorizes distinct functions to be performed by a provider entity. These functions would otherwise have to be performed by the PSO itself. The PSO is obligated to ensure that these delegated activities are properly performed and meet the standards of the appropriate accrediting agency (e.g., the National Committee for Quality Assurance [NCQA]), since the responsibility for these functions remains with the PSO. The plan is obligated to ensure proper performance through a formal oversight process.

While delegation usually follows the transfer of financial risk, PSOs can transfer financial risk with little, if any, delegation of functions. Delegation of substantial financial risk without delegation of some critical administrative functions will deprive the providers of data that are essential to their management of the financial risk as well as their delivery of care. Administrative services that are important to delegate in order to manage financial risk effectively are claims payment, utilization review, and quality improvement.

Accrediting agencies generally are supportive of delegation and feel it is an appropriate practice if there is a good cooperative relationship between the health plan and the contracting provider entities. However, these agencies do not typically favor the delegation of the standards of performance or the evaluation of new technologies. Accrediting agencies require that the delegated providers meet the same standards as imposed upon the health plan. Periodic audits by the PSO are to be expected, and the providers must take care to meet the audit criteria.

Although the approach to delegation may vary, it must be based on a clear understanding by both parties and supported by a detailed written and signed delegation agreement. Open and frequent communication for the development of a mutually beneficial relationship between the health plan and the providers is essential. Critical success factors include

- ongoing cooperation between the PSO and the provider entity
- comfort in sharing clinical and financial information
- compatible and skillful resources in the PSO and provider entity
- efficient and reliable operating systems (processes and technology)
- well-designed reporting and ongoing communication
- delegation processes that are well integrated with the PSO's internal operations
- timely and substantial evaluation, action, and follow-up

CLAIMS PROCESSING

Delegation of claims processing is the cornerstone of successful management and is essential to success. With claims payment, the organization has absolute control of dollars expended and can thus avoid payment errors that are hard to correct (duplicate and unauthorized out-of-network payments). Unfortunately, it is the function that is most difficult for many health plans to delegate.

If the PSO retains responsibility for paying claims, yet the providers are at risk for the dollars, the PSO is, in effect, writing checks with the providers' money. The PSO has less of an incentive to ensure that the claims paid are appropriate and valid.

Claims payment also is essential for obtaining the utilization data used in managing clinical utilization and financial risk. Health plan data that are forwarded to providers in lieu of primary claims data are typically untimely and unreliable.

Providers need to fully understand that it is not easy to pay claims accurately and in a timely manner. In taking the responsibility for the payment of claims, they need to invest in the technology to electronically manage, in a standardized format, many important managed care functions, including

- enrollment
- eligibility
- referral
- certification (precertification and concurrent certification)
- claims submission
- claims status reporting
- claims payment and remittance

CREDENTIALING

Practitioners are selected for health plan participation based upon many factors. Credentialing is the process of collecting and verifying information related to a practitioner's licensure, clinical privileges, history of disciplinary actions and professional liability claims, malpractice coverage, and practice profile. It is an important part of a PSO's provider contracting and network development process. Credentialing is an administrative function that can easily be coordinated between a provider entity and a PSO. Should a PSO delegate credentialing to the providers, the following key questions should be answered:

- Which party is responsible for collecting the data?
- Where are the files kept? Who has access to the information?
- Where is the credentialing function performed?
- Who makes the decisions about including or excluding providers in the provider entity?
- Which party is responsible for follow-up and ongoing communication with the providers?

When credentialing is delegated, providers are responsible for the data collection and verification functions. They also determine participation based on the information gathered. They can accept or reject a physician as they choose, but the health plan will retain the right to reject a physician who has been accepted by the providers. The PSO cannot, however, force the providers to accept a physician they rejected.

Primary control over credentialing allows the providers to choose the practitioners with whom they will share risk. It also allows for the more rapid addition of new physicians to provider panels—avoiding the long delays in reimbursement experienced by new associates awaiting traditional health plan credentialing.

If physician practices are owned or affiliated with a health system and the health system has established a centralized credentialing service, the PSO can utilize the centralized service rather than duplicating the function by separately credentialing the physicians. However, the credentialing entity will have to meet the standards of the most stringent party using it as a credentialing agent. Internet access to databases and electronic application filing will make credentialing less labor intensive and more reliable.

Once a delegated credentialing program is established, the PSO should routinely audit the physician data and set performance parameters that the provider organization will need to maintain to continue to have the delegated responsibility. Credentialing plans should be updated annually, and the delegated relationship should be reviewed on an ongoing basis. If there is sufficient size and activity, certification by NCQA (acting as a credentialing verification organization) may be advantageous. This would eliminate the need for some health plan audits. It is important to note that credentialing activities include the review of the providers' sites (e.g., offices) and medical records.

MEDICAL RECORDS

If the PSO and provider panel jointly account for a significant number of members, it is efficient to coordinate the evaluation of medical records between the PSO and provider entity. This will allow for a uniform and efficient review of the clinical information within the members' medical records. It also reduces the manpower and energy required for multiple audits and decreases the disruptions within physician offices caused by health plan audits.

Medical record review, including all scoring and data analysis, of blind charts at initial credentialing and/or member charts at recredentialing is typically completed by a clinical professional. The reviewer reports back to the physician entity whether the reviewer judged the documentation to be acceptable, unacceptable, or pended. For unacceptable or pended reviews, follow-up is conducted and documented.

The kind of evaluation of the medical records that is usually performed is suggested by the following questions:

- Are all papers secured?
- Is there a place in the record to identify the member?
- Is there a written confidentiality policy for medical records?
- Are the medical records legible?

- Is biographical or personal information complete and included?
- Are allergies prominently noted?
- Is there a list of current problems and medications?
- Are immunizations noted for members 12 years and younger?
- Do progress notes contain the date; complaint or reason for visit; objective findings; history and physical examination; diagnosis; testing, treatments, and medications ordered; and patient instructions?
- Is there a notation regarding follow-up care?
- Are all entries dated and is the provider identified?
- Is information available on advance directives?
- Is one person designated for record maintenance?
- Are medical records and patient charts kept in a fireproof locked cabinet?

UTILIZATION MANAGEMENT

Utilization management may be delegated entirely or may be shared with the PSO. The functions involve the authorization for care and the management of appropriate referrals (physician consultation, postacute care, and outpatient diagnostic tests) and the effective utilization of inpatient days. The structure and detail of the process are variable, but it is essential that the decisions related to appropriateness are timely and consistent with physician oversight. An adequate and well-designed appeals process must be in place for both the physician and the member.

In addition to management function detailed above, the utilization management function involves analysis and presentation of meaningful data to the providers, such as

- acute admissions per 1,000 members
- inpatient days per 1,000 members

- observation days per 1,000 members
- emergency department visits per 1,000 members
- outpatient procedures per 1,000 members
- physician visits per 1,000 members
- prescriptions per 1,000 members

It is by using such data that utilization and level of care issues are identified and addressed. As stated earlier, having primary data that are reliable and can be formatted for maximum impact on the providers is essential. In many cases, traditional health plan data are not available, nor do they ensure thorough care management and clinical data evaluation.

QUALITY IMPROVEMENT

Quality improvement activities do not lend themselves to complete delegation because the health plan is held accountable for the quality studies and statistics for its entire membership. Thus, data from a single provider panel are neither useful nor meaningful to the health plan.

The best approach to a quality improvement program is a collaborative one, with the plan utilizing its data as they relate to the specific provider panel. It is, however, useful and informative to identify and trend quality issues, as well as sentinel events, within the provider panel. The quality issue information can be used during recredentialing. This also allows the providers to identify and address issues before the PSO gets involved, resulting in greater autonomy and credibility for the providers.

The providers should attempt to assume responsibility for managing issues identified by health plan information rather than waiting for the PSO medical director to take the initiative to get involved. It is imperative to establish a credible and cooperative relationship between the provider leadership and the PSO medical director and the related staff. The ability of providers to maintain control of utilization and quality intervention allows clinical and professional decisions to be made by professionals practicing within the member's community rather than at the PSO level.

MEMBER RELATIONS

It is important for PSOs and their provider entities to document the receipt of member complaints. The time frame, the response, and the resolution of each complaint should be documented. The PSO, as well as the delegated provider entity, needs to be able to verify the protocol, the standards, a record of actions taken, the time lines of the actions, and the communication with the member. On an ongoing basis, communication between the PSO, provider entity, and member should be consistent. The delegated relationship between the PSO and the providers should be virtually invisible to the member.

DELEGATION AGREEMENT

It is absolutely essential that there be a clear delegation agreement in writing signed by both parties. It should be very specific and be executed prior to the delegation of responsibilities. The agreement should contain several points to ensure that there is a clear understanding by all parties of the duties and responsibilities of each party:

- The agreement should clearly list the responsibilities of the delegatees.
- The standards by which the services will be judged and which party is ultimately responsible should be clearly stated.
- The monitoring and evaluation process to be used by the PSO, including any evaluation tools, and the frequency of the evaluation process should be clearly addressed.

- The remedies available to the PSO for any deficiencies should be outlined. It should also be clear how long a delegated function would be allowed to be deficient before revocation would occur.
- The plan of action and expected corrective actions (and documentation of their execution) by the delegatees should be clearly documented.
- The contents of the reports and the frequency of the reports to the PSO should be clearly defined. In addition, the protection of proprietary and peer review information should be clearly stated.
- It is important for both the PSO and the delegatees to understand that all delegated functions must be fully integrated into the comparative function of the health plan and fit with the overall operations and oversight of the PSO.

ACCREDITING ENTITIES

There are multiple accrediting agencies that will impose standards on shared and/or delegated services. The NCQA and Joint Commission on Accreditation of Healthcare Organizations (Joint Commission) are two such organizations. Although both organizations aspire to monitor quality, their approaches to accreditation are different.

NCQA accredits and monitors the quality of health plans. It attempts to provide the purchasers of health care information to judge health plans based upon their quality and value.

The NCQA accreditation process is not mandatory. However, over half of the nation's health plans participate in the accreditation activities. It is probable that PSOs will seek the security of NCQA accreditation as well. Just as employers, such as IBM, PepsiCo, USAir, and Ford, look for NCQA accreditation for their employed populations, so will they look for accreditation for their retirees.

NCQA uses 50 different standards that fall into the following six categories:

1. quality management and improvement (40 percent of health plan's score)
2. credentialing and recredentialing (20 percent)
3. members' rights and responsibilities (10 percent)
4. preventive health services (15 percent)
5. utilization management (10 percent)
6. medical records (5 percent)

There are NCQA delegation standards for each function. The degree of delegation is determined by the percentage of the health plan's total membership that is delegated. Once the delegation is determined to be minor (0–29 percent), moderate (30–59 percent), or major (60–100 percent), there is a determination on the subsequent type of oversight by the NCQA.

If the percentage of delegated members is less than 29 percent, then the oversight is minor. There will be oversight of file review of the managed care organization but no evaluation of the delegated entity's process, only of the health plan process. If there is moderate to major delegation, then NCQA not only evaluates the health plan's process but also carefully evaluates the delegated entity's process.

If physicians are part of a network that is also seeking Joint Commission accreditation, they may find themselves faced with different credentialing standards. For instance, with the NCQA standards, if a physician is board certified, the physician's medical school and level of education need to be verified. With Joint Commission accreditation, *all* training must be verified, even if the physician is board certified.

OVERSIGHT AND EVALUATION

If a delegatee is certified by the NCQA in certain functions, then the PSO does not have to reaudit the delegates to make sure that it is functioning up to NCQA standards. It is important to note, however, that the health plan may require and audit for additional standards (over and above the NCQA standards).

There should be a clear outline of the scope of the oversight, the frequency, and the tools being used to evaluate the health plan. There are three stages of evaluation for a PSO in its relationship with a provider entity:

- an evaluation of the delegatee's capacity prior to delegation
- performance evaluations at regular intervals during the delegation (these should be more frequent if the delegatee is inexperienced)
- an annual evaluation of standards

CERTIFICATION

Whereas a health plan may attempt to obtain NCQA approval, no NCQA approval process is available for provider organizations. These organizations may, however, seek certification for select functions.

Over the coming years, provider organizations will face increasing pressure to become certified. By achieving certification, a provider organization will increase its market credibility and gain consumer confidence.

An appropriate place to start in the certification process is utilization management and credentialing. The ability of provider organizations to be certified in these functions gives them great flexibility and allows them to grow at a reasonable pace.

Certification can be very valuable to a large system with multiple contracts. With certification, the system becomes a credentialing verification organization (CVO), and it can then implement central and independent collection of data that can be used by multiple provider groups for a variety of contracts. This not only increases efficiency of contracting but decreases overhead, which is so essential in these days of falling revenue.

CONCLUSION

Delegation of administrative functions from a health plan to a provider organization can be important—and beneficial—to both organizations. It provides flexible, responsive, and appropriate decision making within the local provider community. Obviously, it can save PSO resources, which can be reallocated to other efforts to improve the PSO's competitive position in the market. The providers, on the other hand, gain the control and data needed to manage their resources to the maximum benefit of their patients, and at the same time they have direct control over the financial risk and its consequences.

For such a relationship to work, both organizations must be credible and reliable. They must form a mutually beneficial and trusting relationship, which results in a "win" for the health plan, for the providers, and for the members. The achievement of this type of relationship presents a challenge, but it can produce a professional environment that is attractive and secure for the providers and gives the patients a compassionate and responsive delivery system anchored by the local physician they know and trust. This will necessarily benefit the health plan, because the control is in the hands of the providers and their patients, the two stakeholders who can, and should, shape the health care delivery system.

CHAPTER 9

Branding Strategies: Survival through Differentiation

Barry S. Scheur

The world of managed care and health insurance has come full cycle in the 25-year period since the passage of the HMO Act in 1973. Original health plans were initiated and sponsored largely by groups of providers who believed that there was benefit in combining the financing and risk management functions of traditional health insurance with the delivery of care. Many of the early health plans utilized restrictive networks, making the marketing of their products difficult. Employers often were not willing to offer these new health care organizations as choices in their health care benefit plans, and the early HMO's only market entry strategy was to employ the "strong arm" provisions available to federally qualified HMOs.

This was not marketing; it was forced entry. The only early efforts that bore any resemblance to marketing strategy and sales involved promotion at health fairs, with lots of pavement pounding and education. Advertising and targeted direct mail were not utilized.

In the mid to late 1980s, insurers began taking more than a passing interest in the phenomenon of managed care. Major indemnity companies spent millions of dollars "branding" their identities, such as "The Rock" for Prudential and the "Red Umbrella" for Travelers. Blue Cross plans had developed their own brand identity—the "health care gold standard"—and it was written into union contracts, with the threat of rampant employee dissatisfaction in the event of a benefits changeover.

For these indemnity plans, managed care was a new product. The benefits were more comprehensive, but the access restrictions and care authorizations still made marketing and sales a challenge. Provider-sponsored HMO plans focused on the market consisting of small to medium-size groups, and the vast majority had under 500 lives and competed on price and benefits.

For the most part, health plans had local names, even those that were part of national insurance companies. Brand recognition, and perhaps more importantly brand consumer reliance, was a hoped-for dream.

As quality of care and access to care became the competitive weapons, marketing and promotion began to increase in prominence. Consumer resistance to managed care was overcome through the use of testimonials, and the emphasis was on the "warm fuzzies" of compassion, caring, and commitment. Doctors became health plan spokespersons, and the managed care advertising age was born.

Today, our airwaves, print publications, and mailboxes are dominated by health care solicitations. HMO plans have come to look more and more like indemnity companies, promoting open access, choice of providers, alternative medicine, and tailored benefits. But there is a constantly growing managed care backlash that is based on the rather large gap between sales and brochure promises and the actual mechanics of securing care. Coextensive with these developments has been, over the past five years, the explosion of managed care into the government programs sectors of Medicare and Medicaid, targeting two population segments that are particularly leery of the managed care truth gap and that can exercise great political leverage when necessary.

As the health care pendulum swings away from national insurance companies toward networks of physicians, hospitals, and health care service providers willing to organize care and assume financial risk for so doing, the question of product strategy and branding becomes important.

With the federal government having recently permitted physicians and hospitals to compete for Medicare patients as managed care plans (i.e., with a flat premium) without the necessity of being licensed as state HMOs, the concept of provider-powered marketing now takes center stage. How can these new physician and hospital organizations, lacking huge capital reserves but needing to establish brand awareness and identity, compete against well-established and -financed managed care marketing campaigns? The remainder of this chapter provides the recipe, a simple one, that has been used time and time again to launch physician- and hospital-sponsored products in highly concentrated managed care markets dominated by long-established payers. It first describes the basic elements of product branding and consumer awareness, and then outlines specific proven strategies for health care providers to utilize in grabbing and holding market share.

Readers familiar with Sun Tzu's essays on the art of war will see a lot of similarities between his characterization of this art and the current state of health care marketing and sales product strategy. The art of waging war for covered lives is becoming synonymous with "success in the health care marketplace." There will be survivors, there will be victors, there will be new ground and new boundaries, there will be battles, there will be new alliances, there will be new leaders, and there will be new laws and regulations. It is a brave new traumatizing and chaotic environment where turmoil reigns and the words "strategic" and "planning" might seem oxymoronic. Whatever the parallels are to the art and tactics of warfare—market destabilization, fear mongering about the loss of the patient relationship in a corporately commoditized health care system, or the unveiling of a secret weapon—emerging provider organizations need to know about market survival, market strategy, and the steps needed to objectively evaluate and then improve upon their own competitive position.

Before looking at the definitive market and product-branding strategies that will first destabilize the market and then take away market share from competitors, we need to come to agreement on some basic realities of the health care landscape at the end of the twentieth century.

HEALTH CARE TRENDS AND BUSINESS REALITIES

The power in health care is shifting back to physicians and hospitals and away from the large integrated insurers that have dominated the marketplace for the past decade. Provider networks have realized that their only leverage against the inevitable financial squeeze placed upon them by insurers is to manage the economic risks of and the opportunities for managing care effectively. This trend will be spurred even further by the creation of the PSO option and the ability of a PSO to compete for Medicare lives as a Medicare+Choice plan. Thus, integrated, provider-controlled delivery systems are well positioned, no matter under which name they flourish. As little as four years ago, the acronyms PHO, MSO, and IDS were unknown to even the most prescient health executive. Today, they are part of the common vocabulary, even if their meanings are not always perceived identically by executives who claim to understand the concepts. It is interesting to reflect on the fact that, at a time when we are preaching elimination of duplication and increased consolidation, what we are actually accomplishing is the creation of thousands of new competitors with new products, new networks, and overlapping relationships—and increasing the bewilderment of the customers, for whom we are supposed to be simplifying the system (a system in which they already do not have much faith).

Competitors in all health care sectors (the payer, practice management, and provider network sectors) are consolidating and forming power entities whose value for their investors is expected to be driven by a rapidly rising share price (on whatever exchange) caused by rapid growth in revenues in turn caused by acquisition and consolidation. An organization can grow by fighting and winning the battle for covered lives in a market or it can grow much more easily through geographic or vertical expansion.

The price of the health care products is still a dominant issue but not the only one. There is the necessity of being able to demonstrate and maintain quality and service value, since health care consumers are becoming ever more cynical and educated on how to make choices based on indicators of good outcomes and above-average service.

Having a market niche is essential. Health plans, and even health care institutions, are finding that in order to compete they must capitalize on what they do best—they must eliminate frills, find treatment for their edifice complex (their fixation on bricks and mortar and high-priced technology), and concentrate on what the customer gravitates to and is seduced by. The goal is to woo customers away from long-standing relationships and then find ways of keeping them once they have been captured. A good motto would be, "Know where your strengths lie and deliver the health plan the customer wants." Do not take the approach of trying to deliver the health plan that only you can manage, or that you can afford, or that you want them to have, or, worse yet, the "me too" health plan that mirrors rather than outperforms its competitors.

Physicians, particularly, have a tremendous opportunity to utilize their best market niche in the battle for covered lives: their existing patient relationships. While much has been made of the fact that patients no longer have loyalty to their physicians when more than a few dollars a month is at stake, most patients still want to believe they can have a unique and confidential relationship with a trusted person who will look out for their physical and emotional well-being. Insurers bring size, stability, tradition, and perhaps safety, but they do not bring "warm fuzzies" during a time of illness nor can they be trusted to put medical needs before money.

It is no surprise, then, that long-established insurers that are not provider owned and whose only real relationships with caregivers are one-year contractual arrangements are utilizing caregivers and patient experiences with them as a cornerstone of their promotional and brand identity. All physician- and other provider-based organizations need to do is destroy the credibility of payers by debunking their moral supremacy as "caregivers" and identifying them for what they are—companies that have been able to successfully turn health care into a commodity and then brand it, package it, and sell it. Differentiated branding of "their" care (meaning payer care) and "our" care (meaning provider care) is a weapon that, when used on even large insurers, panics their executives. The reason is simple: insurers do not own the single greatest generators of trust when it comes to the delivery of health care, the practitioners and facilities themselves.

The health care sale is already a complex one, and it will become even more so in the future. Managed care organizations, including provider-sponsored networks, have at least three sets of customers, all of whom must be continually satisfied. The employer or a government entity makes benefits packages available, the consumer selects a package, and a variety of participating caregivers, facilities, and service providers reinforces its value through the way patients get treated. It is logical to believe that provider organizations, whether they be medical groups or networks, will treat patients better, at least from a service perspective (by improving appointment scheduling if nothing else), when they are most effectively supported and served by their own managed care customers.

Adding to the complexity of this world of relationships between caregivers and care sellers is the role of the third-party insurance broker who looks after the insurance needs of business customers. Many managed care organizations have attempted to bypass the inevitable sales commissions by creating competitive sales forces. Other health care plans try to reduce the brokers' commission structure or range of incentives after developing a block of business, believing somehow that the loyalty of the customers will have switched from the insurance broker to the health plan itself. Sometimes this is a correct assumption, but more often it is not!

The role of the media and the importance of promotion and advertising—direct mail, telemarketing, and broadcast distribution—will continue to grow exponentially. Expensive advertising campaigns that promote health plan names and logos are becoming as recognizable as ads for upscale cars and premium beers. In health care, the media truly have become the message, a concept that some people will remember was originally put forth by Marshall McCluhan some 30 years ago; in fact, promotion and marketing expenditures are expected to rise by as much as 500 percent over the next five years. A new entrant into the health care marketing sweepstakes may have to be prepared to spend 25–50 percent of its start-up costs on product development, customer familiarization, and product branding, not to mention the additional costs of sales—and then be prepared to maintain a 20-percent expenditure level for marketing and promotion in the foreseeable future.

In spite of the growing use of increasingly sophisticated marketing and sales approaches, product branding and advertising campaigns in health care are still primitive compared to those in other consumer industries. Product initiatives and ad campaigns are still too often launched without significant input from those segments whose attention is being sought or whose purchasing power is being solicited for redirection. Furthermore, the claims made for health care products are too often put forth without input from those people within the health care company who must deliver on the "promises" being made. For example, physicians participating in a health plan should not have to find out what the plan has promised from the radio, the television, the newspaper, or (horrors of horrors) the patient in an emergency situation. Provider sponsored organizations have a much better opportunity to both educate and inform their constituencies about message, promises, and expectations. There is still a great opportunity for the product branding and promotion strategies of provider networks and provider-owned health plans to take advantage of the lack of creativity and misinformation that too often still remains the standard for the marketing and promotion of managed care.

There will be a continuing provider-payer joust for control that draws the battle lines for patients' or purchasers' loyalty between non-provider-sponsored insurers and provider-controlled networks and organizations. In immature and volatile environments, where managed care is growing in terms of size of enrollment and diversity of products offered, the opportunity to differentiate a provider-driven organization is, and will remain, significant.

Consumers are cynical about managed care because of its failure to deliver on the promises made—cost efficiency, care monitoring, service, and perceived quality. Most of the tarnish has not, however, penetrated to the level of the caregiver. This is one explanation why the health care reform initiative of the first Clinton Administration failed so miserably. Consumers were not willing to accept a reform platform that took great delight in making villains of the very physicians and institutions upon whom they depended for treatment and healing. Health care cost reform has now evolved dramatically into a different kind of political agenda, one where reform will be achieved by allowing provider-sponsored entities to compete for Medicare business (and soon probably commercial and Medicaid business) against the previously upstart but now entrenched (and distrusted) managed care payers. The potential marketing opportunities afforded by the positioning and ad campaign representations that "patients, not dollars, are still our business" or that "we are the people who really make you better, rather than just taking your money" are vast (and frightening for physicians and hospitals to contemplate).

The frequency of encounters with the health care system and the variety of interactions with respect to both the actual care and the services that support the care and the insurance functions make the challenge of delivering value daunting, but the rewards are significant for those provider organizations that can align and then showcase the synergies between quality, operational smoothness, and service excellence. Health care still seems to be a field where the prize remains to be taken in many markets because of the cynicism with which managed care is perceived and because of the scarcity of organizations that have understood the requisites for brand and product success.

The ultimate success, measured in terms of maximized enrollment and customer retention, will be achieved by those health care companies that rethink and reengineer their total business function from both the patient-as-customer and the provider-as-customer perspectives. A relatively poorly perceived market brings with it a wealth of opportunity for those organizations that can simply identify, meet, and then benchmark customer expectations. Hospitals now have valet parking, and physicians and hospitals have made convenience a platform through establishment of satellite offices, but what is the equivalent for managed health care organizations? They had better find out soon or the lessons learned by the institutions and the caregivers will be used to reclaim market supremacy.

Despite the richness of opportunities for caregivers and their supporting institutions to reestablish a significant amount of control through competitive product differentiation and branding, much of the potential will be lost due to constant infighting and turf battling. Unfortunately, physicians as a group have not, for the most part, figured out that it is better to work with an economic unit that supports their common interests than to battle with each other over medical staff privileges or inclusion in networks. Add to this reality the continued level of distrust between physicians and hospitals, and the Wall Street–driven managed care enterprises may still continue to be on top, not because they are entitled to success but because of the pronounced myopia of the organizations directly responsible for actually delivering care. To date, shareholder organizations (as opposed to provider sponsored organizations) engaged in the management and financing of care have had one great priority: managing cost. Provider-controlled companies have a chance to carry out their functions on a higher plain, and one that will doubtless be shown to be more appealing to and dovetail with the needs of business, government, and consumer customers. Quality of care and quality of service will not simply be measured through advertising campaign recitation of customer satisfaction ratings. After all, if people are so satisfied with their health care plans, why is so much attention being paid to the managed care backlash?

Those individuals and organizations whose business and life experiences truly revolve around medical care delivery are in the best position to devise product and marketing strategies that translate the uniqueness of what provider-sponsored health care represents into messages that consumers can understand

and embrace. "From black bag to black box" is not always seen as positive by customers, and providers can capitalize on the view espoused by consumers that managed care results in the depersonalization of medical care delivery. Too many managed care organizations clearly have crossed the line between operating in businesslike manner to operating medicine as a business. This is the specific area of vulnerability for insurers; hence the opportunity for leverage offered to visionary provider-driven organizations and networks. Unmasking the many payers that have come to believe in health care predominantly as a business is the key that will unlock the use of provider-driven market power—if provider organizations and networks are willing to utilize the lessons learned from patient dissatisfaction to their advantage.

MARKETING GUIDELINES

The following guidelines are meant to stimulate creative thinking on how a provider organization can differentiate itself and communicate that difference through the use of advertising and promotion. It is more important that the differentiation be articulable and have a logical basis than that it be 100 percent provable. Many physicians, trained scientifically, are literalists when it comes to communications and marketing. They want unassailable proof, which is lacking for almost any theory.

These guidelines are predicated on a belief system about human nature, the role of communications and advertising in our society, and the likely reactive behavior of competitors. If they do not ring true to you, then your organization may need to be educated about product branding in the "real world."

Perception is reality. What people perceive about a product's value, quality, and shortcomings is more important than the actual comparative performance of the product itself.

When launching a new concept or idea, your first obligation is to get the audience's attention, whatever you have to do to accomplish that. That is why negative disparagement comparison works as an initial marketing strategy, but the overall message must be based on the positive value of the product being sold. Motto: you can shoot at competitors once to wound them, but you have to take them out on your merits and their shortcomings.

Creation of a brand identity is not cheap, nor is it quick. It takes reinforcement over a relatively long period of time. If you want results, expect to have to saturate the market for a while, to the point where the product's superlatives will speak for themselves and carry the branding along even further.

Market and product strategies are not consensus driven, and don't worry about trying to get agreement from those people who are not really involved except as critics of other people's work. If you are unsure of how well something will work, obviously you need data from surveys and focus groups. But gathering anecdotal data from a key group of executives or fearful board members just does not cut it.

A marketing and product differentiation strategy works for a given time period and then has to be updated to deal with new competitive realities in the marketplace. Wheaties may still be the "Breakfast of Champions," but the definition of a champion may have to change. For example, for a long time women athletes were not even featured on Wheaties boxes.

POSSIBLE PROVIDER BRANDING STRATEGIES

The Lowest Price Strategy. The emphasis is on value and low cost—the product you can afford, with no strings attached, simple underwriting, and a "benefits build-up" menu that lets you buy the benefits and services you need. Physicians understand patients—after all, they see them up close and personal every day, and these are the things you tell us you want from your health care program. Examples include alternative medicine, point-of-service care, nonprescription drug benefits, extended nursing home coverage, and supplemental behavioral health coverage.

The Stability Strategy. There will be many new players, but would you hand over your health care to a kid with a chemistry set and a curiosity about explosives? We have the experience. We have the history. We know the market. We understand your medical needs and not just benefits and cost shifting. We put education first. We work with value-added resellers like brokers, and we care about changing your health status for the better and improving health outcomes communitywide.

The Provider-Community Strategy. We have taken care of you as your medical care system since long before insurers and payers got into the for-profit health care game. We are not middlemen inserting ourselves between the care decisions and the patients. We still care, as institutions and health care professionals in this community, about your welfare regardless of cost. You are more than a number, and your convenience and comfort still matter to us. Besides, local providers are involved in medical decision making, not in offering medical recommendations to a higher authority. You must compare what the discounting and packaging of health care within faceless financial empires will mean to you before you make a decision on what to buy. (This is a particularly valuable approach when in a price war that can't be won.)

The "Putting Our Customer First" Strategy. We offer you product flexibility, service guarantees, and low prices. Whatever you want, we will stand and deliver, with less concern about this year's profit than about our long-term relationship.

The "Warm and Fuzzy" Strategy, or Insurer as Caregiver. When my child got sick, they did everything for him and, by implication and suggestion, so will they for you.

This strategy should not be tried without proper preparation. It also needs to be supported by a heavy dose of education about the fact that insurers, while not owning physician and hospital networks, do rent them. By contrast, in provider-sponsored health plans, caregivers are actually in charge of decisions.

The David vs. Goliath Strategy. We are smaller, we are more personal, we care. In short, you are not patient no. 120703. You have an appointment when it is scheduled, your time is valuable, and our average encounter is not just seven minutes long.

The Fear-of-Oversize Strategy. What you get from big alliances of purchasers and payers is freeze-dried, assembly-line health care. Think of what you get from frozen food packagers, automobile manufacturers, and long-distance phone service providers. You will have to make changes more often if you sign up with insurers and managed care companies that appeal to the God of Profit and Shareholders first. And think about what it means when health care gets treated as a warranty item; you might well be told that the particular body adjustment or surgery you need is outside the warranty this year because of the company's need to make more money.

The Quality Strategy. We will airlift you when the appropriate care is not available. We have taken the time to build the best network: it includes teaching institutions, its designated arbiters of quality are certified, and it offers full convenience. Quality costs a little more, but, as providers and caregivers, we believe you should have it and we have done everything we can to offer it to you. When it is your life that is under consideration, you should think seriously about paying for it.

The "We Are Business People" Strategy. We are here as your business partner, and we look at business the same way you do—as an appropriate balancing of price and value. In fact, as providers, we know the right balance better than a disinterested insurer would.

The Deemphasis on Insurance and the Emphasis on Care Strategy. You do not want to think about purchasing insurance; you are really buying peace of mind and security.

The Hardheaded Comparison Strategy. When you look behind the advertising, here is what we give in benefits and in network capabilities. Here are our testimonials. Now here is what you may get from others.

Use facts about competitors' disenrollment of patients and use of dollars as a blunt instrument, and then deliver the message in as high profile a manner as possible, preferably through television.

The Perpetuation Strategy. We are health care providers first, and this is how we make our living. We are not here for a short-term investment, especially where the future of your and your family's lives are involved.

CONCLUSION

Provider sponsored organizations are in the unique position to capitalize on their ownership. By promoting their provider orientation, they can create unique market and product-branding programs. These programs can take advantage of consumers' widespread cynicism regarding insurance-based managed care companies and perpetuate the notion that provider-based health plans know patients better, care for patients more, cost less, and deliver higher quality care.

APPENDIX A

Medicare+Choice Core Application for Federally Waived Provider Sponsored Organizations

Department of Health and Human Services
Health Care Financing Administration
Center for Health Plans and Providers
Health Plan Purchasing and Administration Group

JUNE 1998

Source: Reprinted from http://www.hcfa.gov/medicare/apps.htm

INTRODUCTION

Preparation of the Application

This computer-assisted format is for IBM compatible personal computers using WordPerfect 6.1 for Windows and Microsoft Excel. The diskette file README.WPD contains important information such as last-minute changes and a list of files on the diskette. Please see the technical instructions included within this form (or the separate file TECHINST.WPD) for working on the application.

Entities That May Use This Application

An entity may use this application if it meets the Provider Sponsored Organizations (PSO) definition in §1855(d) and in 42 CFR 422.350 through .356 of the Social Security Act and has **a waiver from the Health Care Financing Administration (HCFA) of the State licensure requirement that is a Medicare + Choice prerequisite for other types of organizations.** A PSO is defined as a public or private entity, established or organized and operated by a health care provider or group of affiliated health care providers who:

- control the PSO,
- directly provide a substantial proportion of health care items and services under the Medicare contract, and
- share, in the case of affiliated providers, substantial financial risk.

This definition and related requirements are set out in the above cited regulations published April 14, 1998 in the Federal Register.[See section below on waivers.]

Please see the PSO decision flowcharts that immediately follow this section of the application to help determine if your organization meets definitional requirements of a Federally

Waived PSO. There are two flowcharts. The first reviews the process for a single health care provider that operates a PSO. The second flowchart reviews the process for a group of affiliates that operate a PSO. Organizations that do not meet the PSO definition and related requirements **should not** use this Medicare+Choice application.

A second category of organization that must use this application are organizations that are licensed by the State in which they operate and want to meet the lower minimum enrollment standards established for PSOs by law. Other Medicare + Choice contractors must have 5,000 enrollees if they operate in an urban area, 1,500 enrollees in a rural area. However, PSOs are permitted a lower minimum enrollments of 1,500 for urban PSOs and 500 for rural PSOs. State licensed entities applying for a M+C contract could be approved by HCFA with the lower enrollment standard **if** the organization qualifies as a PSO. The organization must meet the definition and related requirements and submit this PSO application with one modification—the financial chapter of the HMO/PPO core application must be substituted for the financial chapter of this application. A State licensed organization does not need a waiver and must meet State solvency requirements, not Federal PSO solvency standards.

Time line: Applicants who wish to begin operation as a Medicare+Choice contractor by January 1, 1999 must have their contract applications approved by HCFA by December 31, 1998. Applicants who wish to begin enrolling Medicare beneficiaries during 1998 as a Medicare+Choice contractor must meet all applicable Medicare+Choice regulations. This later option will likely require organizations to submit a two-part application: (1) this "core" application, and (2) a supplemental application that will be released after HCFA's publication of Medicare+Choice regulations.

NOTE: This core Federally waived PSO application should be completed and sent to HCFA for review. Later, any supplemental information that the published regulation requires can be submitted to update the application.

Waiver of State Licensure Requirement for PSOS

A fundamental requirement of the Medicare+Choice program is that a Medicare+Choice organization must be organized and licensed under state law as a risk-bearing entity eligible to offer health insurance or health benefits coverage in each state in which it offers a Medicare+Choice plan. However, §1855(a)(2) of the Act and implementing regulations at 422.370 establishes an exception to this general rule by allowing a PSO to obtain a federal waiver from the state licensure requirement if it meets one of four criteria specified in the Act:

- The state failed to complete action on a licensing application within 90 days;
- The state denied the licensing application based on discriminatory treatment;
- The state denied the licensing application based on the organization's failure to meet solvency requirements, and there is a difference between the state's solvency requirements and the federal solvency requirements to be established through a negotiated rulemaking process.
- The state licensing authority has notified the organization in writing that it will not accept their license application.

PSO applicants that are not licensed under state law as risk-bearing entities but meet other applicable requirements must submit waiver requests to HCFA and receive waiver approval, before submitting application materials. (There are separate PSO waiver request and application forms.) **HCFA will not begin reviewing PSO Medicare+Choice applications until the waiver request is approved.** Application for a waiver of the licensure requirement may be made until November 1, 2002 and the approved waiver is effective for a nonrenewable 36-month period. The waiver request form is available on HCFA's Internet web site: http://www.hcfa.gov/medicare/mplusc.htm#waiver.

Reference Materials

Information requested in this application is based on Public Law 105-33, the Balanced Budget Act of 1997. The applicant should be familiar with the following materials:

1. Public Law 105-33, the Balanced Budget Act of 1997, Subtitle A—Medicare+Choice Program
2. *Federal Register* notices: RIN 0938-AI25 9/23/1997; RIN 0938-AI45 1/20/1998; RIN 0938-AI60 4/14/98; RIN 0938-AI83 5/7/98.
3. Documents found under the Balanced Budget link on HCFA's Internet Web Site (http://www.hcfa.gov)
4. Operational Policy Letters, Physician Incentive Plan disclosure forms and instructions, and Adjusted Community Rate information are available at HCFA's web site—*http://www.hcfa.gov/medicare/mgdcar1.htm*
5. HMO National Data Reporting Requirements (NDRR Annual and Quarterly Statements). This information is available from the National Association of Insurance Commissioners, 120 West 12th Street, Kansas City, Missouri 64105, (816) 842-3600.

GENERAL INSTRUCTIONS

To clarify any question, refer to the statutory or regulatory citation upon which it is based. A statutory citation is provided after most questions.

A completed application includes:

1. Cover Sheet with the appropriate signatures
2. Table of Contents for the Narrative part
3. Table of Contents for Documents part
4. Narrative part, with each question copied and brief and precise answers, divided into chapters
5. Documents part, arranged by chapters, that follows the Narrative. Pre-printed materials, such as marketing bro-

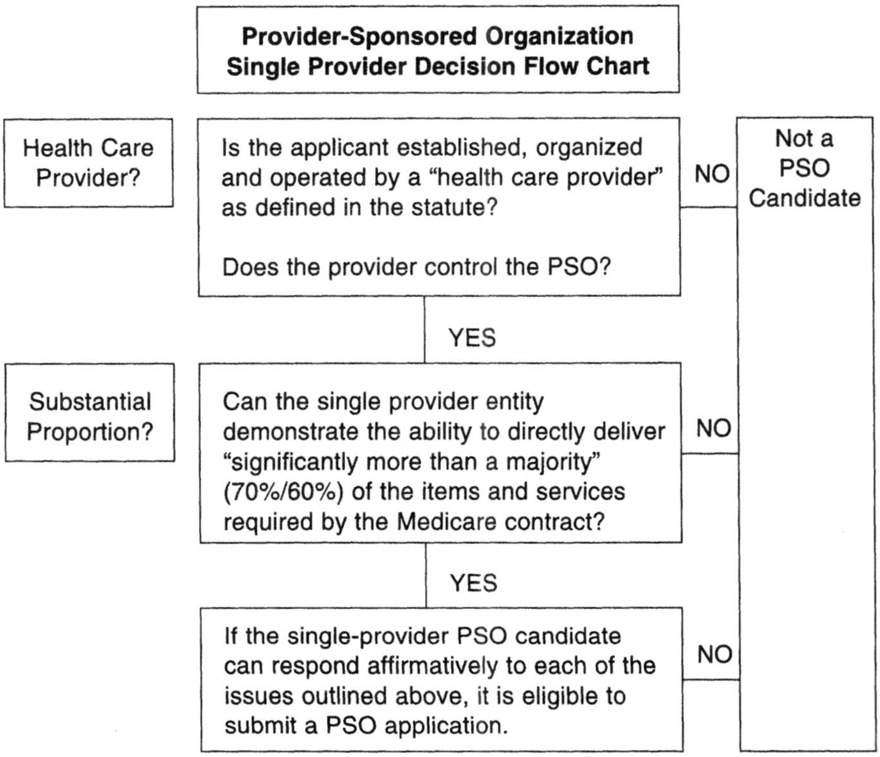

chures and booklets, may be inserted in envelopes in the appropriate places in the application. The envelope should be numbered as a single page.

Number all pages consecutively from the Narrative through the entire Documentation part. Use a page number when referring to any document. If pages must be inserted after numbering has been completed, additional pages may be noted by A, B, C, etc.

TABLES: Tables that are separate files should be placed in the Document part of the application, organized by chapter, as directed in the Narrative sections.

Provider-Sponsored Organization
Decision Flow Chart

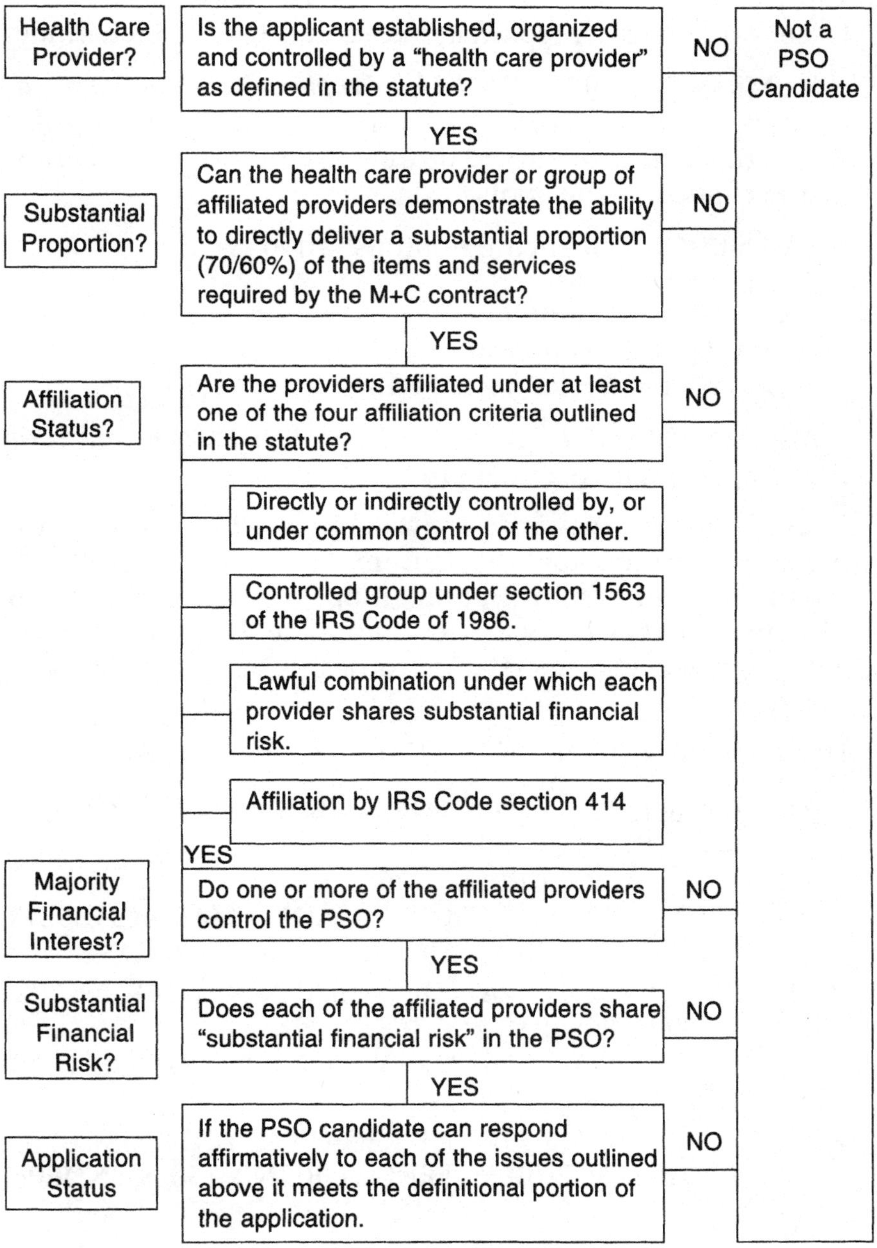

PRINTING AND BINDING: Both sides of the page should be used. Tabs should be inserted for each chapter of the Narrative and Documents parts. Each copy should be put in three-ring loose-leaf binders. A typical application is three 3 inch binders.

NUMBER OF COPIES: *Send 3 hard copies of your application and 2 diskette copies to the address below.* Include 1 diskette copy of the ACRP; the hard copy should be included in the Financial Documents chapter of the application.

Health Care Financing Administration
CHPP/HPPA
4-23-07 North Building
7500 Security Boulevard
Baltimore, Maryland 21244-1850

Also, send *two hard copies of the application and one diskette copy* to the appropriate regional office.

ASSISTANCE: Assistance is available to all applicants in the preparation of this application from the staff of the Health Plan Purchasing and Administration group. You may call (410) 786-1106 to request assistance. The appropriate HCFA regional office will provide assistance relating to health services delivery and Medicare.

HCFA REGIONAL MEDICARE HMO COORDINATORS

RO I JOHN F. KENNEDY FEDERAL BUILDING, ROOM 2375, BOSTON, MA 02203
TELEPHONE: 617-565-1264
STATES: CONNECTICUT, MAINE, MASSACHUSETTS, NEW HAMPSHIRE, RHODE ISLAND, VERMONT

RO II 26 FEDERAL PLAZA, ROOM 3800, NEW YORK, NY 10278
TELEPHONE: 212-264-3661
STATES: NEW JERSEY, NEW YORK, PUERTO RICO, VIRGIN ISLANDS

RO III HCFA, OFFICE OF THE REGIONAL ADMINISTRATOR, SUITE 216, PUBLIC LEDGER BLDG, 150 S. INDEPENDENCE MALL WEST, PHILADELPHIA, PA 19106

TELEPHONE: 215-861-4159
STATES: DELAWARE, DISTRICT OF COLUMBIA, MARYLAND, PENNSYLVANIA, VIRGINIA, WEST VIRGINIA

RO IV ATLANTA FEDERAL CENTER- 4th floor, 61 FORSYTH ST., SW, SUITE 4T20, ATLANTA, GA 30303
TELEPHONE: 404-730-3782
STATES: ALABAMA, FLORIDA, GEORGIA, KENTUCKY, MISSISSIPPI, NORTH CAROLINA, SOUTH CAROLINA, TENNESSEE

RO V 105 WEST ADAMS 15th FL., CHICAGO, IL 60603-6201
TELEPHONE: 312-353-5737
STATES: ILLINOIS, INDIANA, MICHIGAN, MINNESOTA, OHIO, WISCONSIN

RO VI 1301 YOUNG STREET, Room 713 & 833, DALLAS, TX 75202
TELEPHONE: 214-767-4455
STATES: ARKANSAS, LOUISIANA, OKLAHOMA, NEW MEXICO, TEXAS

RO VII NEW FEDERAL OFFICE BUILDING, ROOM 235, 601 EAST 12th ST., KANSAS CITY, MO, 64106
TELEPHONE: 816-426-5033
STATES: IOWA, KANSAS, MISSOURI, NEBRASKA

RO VIII FEDERAL OFFICE BUILDING, 1961 STOUT ST, ROOM 522, DENVER, CO 80294
TELEPHONE: 303-844-6149, EXT 240
STATES: COLORADO, MONTANA, NORTH DAKOTA, SOUTH DAKOTA, UTAH, WYOMING

RO IX DIVISION OF MEDICARE, 75 HAWTHORNE STREET #401, SAN FRANCISCO, CA 94105-3901
TELEPHONE: 415-744-3621
STATES: ARIZONA, CALIFORNIA, GUAM, HAWAII, NEVADA, SAMOA

RO X 2201 6th AVENUE, BLANCHARD BUILDING, RX-44, SEATTLE, WA 98121
TELEPHONE: 206-615-2371
STATES: ALASKA, IDAHO, OREGON, WASHINGTON

PUBLIC REPORTING BURDEN: These forms are voluntary and not required by HCFA. However to assure consistent information from applicants and an efficient review process, you are encouraged to use these forms.

TECHNICAL INSTRUCTIONS

Using the computer assisted format, you will need only to fill in responses in the Narrative part and the applicable tables. For the Documents part, you will need to assemble the documents as directed within the application form and General Instructions. The Documents part does not have a computer assisted format.

SYSTEM REQUIREMENTS: An IBM or compatible personal computer with high density floppy drive, DOS 5.0 or later, WordPerfect 6.1 for Windows and Excel spreadsheet.

The computerized application was designed using a Hewlett Packard Laserjet Series III laser printer and a 12-point Times New Roman *proportionally-spaced* font. Other printers may have comparable fonts such as Times Roman, Dutch 801 Roman, Charter, etc., and these fonts should be suitable, but may format pages slightly differently.

INSTALLATION: To begin, install the electronic version of the application onto your computer's hard disk. You should be in WordPerfect for Windows, in the WPDOCS directory; put the application diskette into the floppy drive, and proceed as follows:

Select **File** from main menu bar; select **Open** from the file menu; you should be in C drive

Select **File Options** from the "Open File" dialog box

Select **Create Directory**

Name the directory **M+CHOICE**, select **Create** (you are now in "Open File" dialog box)

Select the drive the diskette is in (usually a:)

Select all files by holding down the **Control key**, then pressing the **forward slash key (/)**

Select **File Options/Copy/In the dialog box,**

at **To, type in c:\WPWIN61\WPDOCS\M+CHOICE** or whatever path your system requires; select **Copy**

COMPLETION OF THE APPLICATION: After installation, the next step is the completion of the application itself on the computer's hard disk within the \M+CHOICE directory.

The files supplied are WordPerfect documents or Excel spreadsheets. See the README file for a description of each file. Also, see the introduction to the application for a description of who should use this form.

To insert your responses in the Narrative chapters, simply position the cursor at the appropriate point for answering the question, and type in the answer. The rest of the application will "bump down" as you type, providing you as much space as needed.

Most tables are provided as separate files on the disk and should be filled in at their separate location. These are coded for small print size. (See Table Management below.) The Narrative sections instructs you on where to place hard copies.

Be sure to resave the document frequently as you progress.

TABLE MANAGEMENT: Most tables direct that a separate table be submitted for each county you have requested for your Medicare geographic area. If you need copies of a table, you should create multiple blank tables within the same file, being sure to place a hard page break between each table. Save the entire file, now containing two or more tables, with the original file name.

Repeat this process each time you need multiple tables within a single file.

PAGINATION is completely automatic within the Narrative part, so the user should not attempt to type in page numbers as ordinary text.

A NARRATIVE TABLE OF CONTENTS at the beginning of the application is created or updated every time you generate the Table of Contents. (see instructions below) You should create or update the Table of Contents as the last step before actually printing the application for submission.

After you have created a Table of Contents within a document, any subsequent editing, no matter how minor, may alter the page numbering in the Table. For that reason, before you print your final version, regenerate a final Table of Contents.

PRINTING THE APPLICATION FOR SUBMISSION:

Generate the Table of Contents for the Narrative part:

Select **Tools/ Table of Contents/ Generate/ OK**

To add the page numbers for the Documents table of contents, place cursor at the end of each line (using the End key) and type in the page number. Do not press ENTER, just place the cursor at the end of the next line for the next page entry.

Save the end result as XXXXXXXX.APP, with the Xs being an abbreviated health plan name.

When you are ready to submit your application, copy all files from the M+CHOICE directory on your hard disk to an empty diskette. Be certain not to further edit any file, either on hard disk or diskette to assure that the printed copy is identical to the diskette copy.

Submit both the diskette and hard copies as directed in the general instructions. Please clearly label the diskette with the plan name, date, and type of application.

GENERAL GUIDELINES FOR SUCCESS: Throughout the application, there are references to documents that are separate files on disk. Most of these files should be printed and placed in the hard copy of the application as directed, usually in a Documents chapter. However, simply leave the files as individual files on the diskette. Do not integrate the files into the application file on the diskette.

- *Each file deals with a specific topic only. Don't append material to any file that belongs elsewhere.*
- *Edit each file under its own file name*
- *The files supplied have both visible and invisible WordPerfect codes. Don't delete any of these codes. Don't attempt to replace these files with new ones of your own creation (the codes will be lost).*
- *Pagination is automatic in the Narrative part; do not attempt to insert page numbers as text.*

This procedure is harder to describe than to perform—it is not as complicated as it may seem!

THE APPLICATION FORM FOLLOWS THIS PAGE
DO NOT SUBMIT THE PREVIOUS PAGES
IN THE PRINTED COPY OF YOUR APPLICATION

<table>
<tr><td colspan="2">HCFA-xxx-x   OMB No. xxxx-xxxx</td></tr>
<tr><td colspan="2">CENTER FOR HEALTH PLANS AND PROVIDERS
HEALTH PLAN PURCHASING AND ADMINISTRATION
MEDICARE+CHOICE APPLICATION</td></tr>
<tr><td colspan="2">TYPE OF MEDICARE+CHOICE CONTRACT

FEDERALLY WAIVED PROVIDER SPONSORED ORGANIZATION</td></tr>
<tr><td>NAME OF LEGAL ENTITY SUBMITTING MEDICARE+CHOICE APPLICATION

TRADE NAME (if different)</td><td>MAILING ADDRESS</td></tr>
<tr><td colspan="2">CEO OR EXECUTIVE DIRECTOR, (if different from above individual)</td></tr>
<tr><td>NAME AND TITLE

TELEPHONE NUMBER</td><td>MAILING ADDRESS</td></tr>
<tr><td>APPLICANT CONTACT PERSON:
NAME
TITLE
ADDRESS

TELEPHONE
E-MAIL
FAX</td><td>CORPORATE STATUS

For profit___ Not for profit__

URBAN/RURAL STATUS

Urban___ Rural___</td></tr>
<tr><td colspan="2">I certify that all information and statements made in this application are true, complete, and current to the best of my knowledge and belief and are made in good faith.</td></tr>
<tr><td>Signature, CEO/Executive Director</td><td>Date</td></tr>
<tr><td>Signature, Board/Trustee Chairman</td><td>Date</td></tr>
</table>

NARRATIVE PART
TABLE OF CONTENTS

The table of contents for the completed application is placed after the cover sheet.

For computerized application users: each chapter and subsection title within the Narrative section is marked for automatic generation of the table of contents on this page. That table appears below with page numbering that reflects a "blank" application. The numbers will change when you generate the table again for the completed application. Please follow the directions in the Technical Instructions to generate the table for the Narrative Section. Note that the table of contents for the Documents part is not generated automatically, and is to be manually filled in after the table for the Narrative.

DOCUMENTS TABLE OF CONTENTS

For computerized application users: To add the page numbers for the Documents table of contents, place cursor at the end of each line (using the End key) and type in the page number. Do not press ENTER, just place the cursor at the end of the next line for the next page entry.

GENERAL INFORMATION

I. *GENERAL*

A. Briefly describe the Medicare+Choice applicant in terms of its history and its present operations. Cite significant aspects of its current financial, marketing, general management, and health services delivery activities. (Do not include information requested in the Legal Entity section.) Indicate if the applicant has been a Medicare risk or cost-based contractor under §1876 or §1833 of the Social Security Act. (§1857(c)(4)). Indicate affiliate experience with the Medicare program.

B. *Medicare Contract Information:* Please complete the Medicare Set-up forms and place them in the Documents part. **Be sure to sign pages, as indicated.**

These forms are in separate WordPerfect file (setup97.mcr) on the disk. [Complete this table in its file on the disk and place the hard copy in the Documents part.]

II. *KEY MANAGEMENT STAFF*

A. In the table below, indicate the individuals responsible for the key management functions of the entity.

PSO Staff Function	*Name*	*Title*	*Employed By*	*% of Time for PSO*
Executive				
Medical Director				
Utilization Review				
Finance				
Marketing				
Medicare Coordinator				
Management Information Systems				
Other				

B. In the Documents part, provide brief position descriptions and resumes for the individuals listed above.

III. *MANAGEMENT INFORMATION SYSTEM (MIS)*

Describe the use of the MIS for day-to-day management of the key plan functions of the PSO, as well as long-term planning. Provide a list of the key reports with a brief description of each. Have MIS reports available on-site for evaluation by HCFA staff.

IV. *GEOGRAPHIC AREA—§1852(c)(1)*

Clearly describe the requested service area in terms of geographic subdivisions such as counties, cities or townships. If not a full county, zip codes must be provided. Provide a detailed map (with a scale) of the complete geographic area clearly showing the boundaries, main traffic arteries, any physical barriers such as mountains and rivers. Show location of health plan ambulatory and inpatient facility providers and suppliers who will serve Medicare members. Show on this map the mean travel time from six points on the geographic area boundary to the nearest ambulatory and institutional services site. The PSO should provide access to inpatient and primary care services that is within 30 minutes or 30 miles of beneficiaries' residence or within the normal pattern of care for that community.

PSO STRUCTURE AND DEFINING REQUIREMENTS

I. *PSO MODEL TYPE AND PSO PROVIDERS—§422.350(b)*

A PSO is established and operated by a single provider or a group of affiliated providers. Individuals and entities must qualify as health care providers, as defined by the PSO regulations. Check one of the two blanks below and follow instructions for the model selected.

___A. Single Provider— A single provider model PSO is a legal entity or a component (line of business) of a legal entity that is able to provide a comprehensive set of services through the physicians, hospital(s), and other providers of the entity's health care system.. (See also "Substantial Proportion.")

1. Describe the structure of the entity and its health care system, including the health care providers and suppliers that are part of the legal entity. (Charts may be used to support this submission.)
2. Identify the provider components (e.g. physician practices, hospitals, skilled nursing facilities, etc.) of the entity that will participate in the PSO.

___B. Affiliated Provider (§422.354) —The affiliated provider model PSO is an entity composed of health care providers that have affiliated in one or more of the following ways:

a. Directly or indirectly controlled by, or under common control of the other,
b. Lawful combination under which each provider shares substantial financial risk for the PSO operations,
c. Controlled group under section 1563 of the IRS code of 1986,
d. Affiliated by section 414 of IRS code of 1986.

1. Describe the structure of the entity and its health care system. (Charts may be used to support this submission.)
2. Describe the affiliation arrangement among the PSO providers. If affiliated by either B.a. or B.b. above, include in the Documents part information that substantiates the affiliation or refer us to any such information included elsewhere in the application, including articles of incorporation, by-laws, binding legal agreements between or among affiliates, and other relevant materials. If affiliated by either B.c. or B.d., provide supporting information to substantiate the PSO's or entity's standing with the IRS.

Complete the "List of Affiliated Health Care Providers" table (affilpro.tbl). [Complete this table in its file on the disk and place the hard copy in the Documents part.]

3. For each affiliate that is a health care provider entity (as defined in regulation), list and describe the ownership or controlling parties of the provider entity. Identify and describe any significant factors that could influence control over the health care provider entity.

4. Describe any mechanisms that will be in place to maintain the relationship of affiliated providers (in good standing) with the PSO. Are there penalties or provisions that deter affiliated providers (in good standing) from terminating their relationship with the PSO?

II. *CONTROL AND GOVERNANCE—§422.352(a)(3)*

A PSO must be under the control of the health care provider in the single provider model or, in the second model, under the control of one or more of the affiliated providers. Control is the direct or indirect influence over the actions and policies of the PSO, regardless of whether the organization is nonprofit or for-profit. Thus, PSO providers should control significant decisions and governance of the organization. For example, the PSO single provider/affiliated providers should have majority ownership in a for-profit corporation; majority membership in a nonprofit, member model corporation; or be the controlling party of a nonprofit, nonmember model PSO. In addition, in each of these organizational structures, the single provider/affiliated providers should control the governing body of the PSO.

A. List the owners, members, stakeholders, and/or controlling parties of the PSO, or the legal entity of which the PSO is a component. Give addresses and phone numbers for each. Identify the provider in the single provider model or any affiliated providers in the affiliated model PSO by inserting their Affiliated Provider Letter from the "List of Affiliated Health Care Providers" table in parenthesis after each name.

B. Complete the following table that lists the parties that have loaned, invested, donated, or otherwise contributed 5 percent or more of the total amount of funds used to capitalize the PSO, or the legal entity of which the PSO is a component. Identify affiliated providers by inserting their Affiliated Provider Letter from the "List of Affiliated Health Care Providers" table in parenthesis after each party. For each listed party, give the percent loaned, invested, donated, or otherwise contributed. Give addresses and telephone numbers for each.

Name of Individual(s) Organizaitons	*Address/Telephone Number*	*Percent Contributed*

C. Complete the following table that lists the members of the governing body (e.g., Board of Directors) of the PSO or the legal entity of which the PSO is a component. For affiliated provider model PSOs, identify the board members who represent affiliated providers by inserting their Affiliated Provider Letter from the "List of Affiliated Health Care Providers" table in parenthesis after each name.

D. How was the governing body initially appointed/elected and how are appointments or elections made on an ongoing basis? (Is the governing body self-perpetuating or is another method, or a combination of methods, used

Governing Body Member Name	*Title*	*Employed By*

to appoint board members?) Identify whether any PSO provider is appointed by an individual or entity that is not an affiliated provider. Describe the powers of any individual or entity other than an affiliated provider in relation to the governing body.

E. Describe voting policies of the governing body. Identify any decisions that are made by other than a majority vote). Describe any significant voting policy/right of members, shareholders, etc. Identify any significant decisions that are made by members, shareholders, etc., by other than a majority vote.

F. Answer the following questions. Provide documentation or a reference to specific citations in documents submitted elsewhere as part of this application (e.g. contracts, by-laws, etc.), to substantiate your responses.

   1. How will the PSO's budget be determined? Who will have final authority to approve the PSO's budget?

   2. Who will have the authority to monitor the compliance of each affiliated provider with the directives of the PSO?

   3. Who will have the authority to enter the PSO into binding contracts? Can they obligate all affiliated providers to the contracts of the PSO?

4. Who will have the authority to hire and fire the chief executive officer of the PSO?
5. Who will have the responsibility to allocate the income and enterprise risk of the PSO? By what process will they decide upon the allocation of income and enterprise risk?
6. Describe the mechanisms in place to resolve disputes between the PSO and its affiliated providers, and disputes between affiliated providers and other owners, members or interested parties (e.g. investors, shareholders, etc.).
7. Describe any significant veto authority, reserve powers, or other limits on the PSO's authority. Include descriptions of limitations in any contract or debt instrument.
8. What provisions are there for an orderly transition in the event an affiliated provider terminates its relationship with the PSO? Describe provisions for continued compliance with the substantial proportion requirement, risk-sharing, and control of the PSO.

III. *SUBSTANTIAL PROPORTION OF SERVICES—§422.352(b)*

The health care provider in a single-provider model PSO, or the affiliated providers in the second model of PSO, must provide a substantial proportion of the services furnished under the contract. PSOs which serve urban areas must provide through the PSO provider, or affiliated providers, 70% of the Medicare services furnished under the M+C contract. For rural PSOs, as defined in regulation, the standard is 60%. At application, this standard must be met through estimated PSO expenditures. However, after the contract is in effect, the substantial proportion standard will be measured through the PSO's expenditure experience.

A. Complete the Substantial Proportion Calculation Worksheet. This table is a separate file *subsprop.xls;* complete the table in its file on the disk and place a hard copy in the Documents part. Instructions for the table are at the end of this chapter.

B. Describe how the PSO will meet this requirement on an ongoing basis after the Medicare contract is in effect. Reference any supporting documentation found elsewhere in this application, such material as affiliated provider contract language that ensures access and availability of services to the PSO enrollees, enrollment projections and available capacity within the PSO, utilization management protocols, plans for maintaining compliance with anticipated expansions, etc.

IV. *SUBSTANTIAL FINANCIAL RISK—§422.356(a)*

For PSOs that are the affiliated provider model, each affiliated provider must share in the financial risk of the PSO enterprise. The risk must be at a level that is "substantial" for the particular provider. Permissible risk sharing arrangements include: 1) agreement by a health care provider (such as a medical group, IPA, or hospital) to accept a capitation payment for each Medicare enrollee of the PSO; 2) agreement by a provider to accept as payment a predetermined percent of the PSO's premium; 3) use of financial incentives, such as withholding a portion of compensation (to be used to cover the losses of the PSO or, if utilization goals are met, redistributed among the affiliates) or predetermined budgets and utilization targets ; 4) or other mechanisms that demonstrate risk sharing (e.g. significant capital investment). However, risk arrangements where the provider is at financial risk for its own items and services, and not the financial risks of the PSO (including losses incurred by other PSO affiliated provider), do not meet this requirement.

A. For each affiliated provider, describe as appropriate the compensation arrangement and/or risk-sharing arrangement with the PSO, and level of risk with the PSO. Include in the Documents part copies of contracts between the PSO and its affiliated health care providers or among affiliated health care providers which demonstrate these arrangements or reference any such documents included elsewhere in this application.

B. Describe any risk-sharing arrangements among affiliated providers. Describe how PSO losses or gains will be distributed among the affiliated providers. Include copies of contracts that substantiate these arrangements or reference any such documents included elsewhere in this application.

V. *HCFA WAIVER—§422.370*

Provide in the Documents part a copy of the HCFA waiver for applicants who are not organized and licensed under state law.

INSTRUCTIONS FOR PSO TABLES

affilpro.tbl List of Affiliated Health Care Providers Table

1. **Column One:** List the health care provider and/or group of affiliated providers that will provide at least 70% (60% rural PSOs) of the Medicare items and services. Use the letter assigned to each name as the identifier of the provider on the *"Substantial Proportion Calculation Worksheet"* and as required on *HSD tables 1—5*. If the PSO is a single provider model, list the PSO as affiliate A.
2. **Column Two:** Provide the principal location of each.
3. **Columns Three and Four:** Provide a contact person and telephone number.
4. **Column Five:** With reference to footnote one under the table, specify the basis of PSO affiliation for each provider.

Insert the number, 1-4, that corresponds to the basis of affiliation.

5. **Column Six:** Provide the page number of this application where the affiliation basis for each provider is documented.

subsprop.xls Substantial Proportion Calculation Worksheet

1. **Column One: Medicare Covered Benefits** This column lists the categories of the Medicare covered benefits that all PSOs are required to provide. For non-rural PSOs, 70% of these services must be delivered directly by the PSO or its affiliated providers. Rural PSOs must deliver 60% of these services through the PSO or its affiliated providers.
2. **Column Two: Percent of Total Expenses** Enter projected expenditures for each Medicare covered benefit category as a percentage of total expenditures for all Medicare covered benefits. Enter all percentages in decimal form. For example, if it is projected that inpatient hospital expenses will account for 40% of the Medicare covered benefit expenditures, enter .40. These projections should be reasonable, reflect expenditure patterns of other M+C plans in the PSO's service area and the Medicare program in general, and be consistent with the PSO's expenditure projections in the Financial Plan and the Adjusted Community Rate Proposal. For a listing of 1996 Medicare expenditures by service as a percentage of total Medicare service expenditures, please refer to the "1996 Medicare Service Expenditures Table"included as the second work sheet on the *subprop.xls* file.
3. **Columns Three to Twelve (labeled A—I): Percent of Expenses for Each Medicare Covered Benefit Delivered by Affiliates** Please provide an estimate of the percentage of total expenditures to be provided by the PSO and/or each PSO affiliate for each Medicare covered

benefit category. The letters at the heading of each column (A—I) correspond with the letters for each affiliated provider on the "List of Affiliated Health Care Providers Table." Please list affiliated providers accordingly. For example, if affiliate "A" will account for 50% of Inpatient Hospital Service expenditures, enter .50 in the "Inpatient Hospital Service" row of the "Affiliated Provider A" column.

If the PSO has affiliated providers past the letter I, please include them on additional copies of the "Substantial Proportion Calculation Worksheet." Provide the sub-total percentage of each Medicare covered benefit category provided by the affiliated providers included on additional copies of this worksheet in the column marked "All Others."

4. **Column Thirteen: Percent Benefit** This column contains protected formulas. It calculates the total percentage of expenditures projected to be delivered by all affiliated providers for each Medicare covered benefit category.

5. **Column Fourteen: Percent Medicare** This column contains protected formulas. It converts the projected percentage of expenditures to be delivered by affiliates for each Medicare covered benefit category into a percentage of total expenditures for all Medicare covered benefits. For example, if Inpatient Hospital expenses are projected to account for 40% of all Medicare covered benefit expenditures and affiliates are projected to deliver 50% of inpatient hospital expenses, then the percentage of total expenditures for all Medicare covered benefits projected for affiliates providing hospital benefits is 20% (40% x 50%). The cell at the bottom of the column labeled, "Estimated Proportion of Medicare Covered Benefits to be Delivered by Affiliated Providers" is also a protected formula. It calculates the sum of this column. To meet the substantial proportion requirement, this cell must equal at least 70% for non-rural PSOs and at least 60% for rural PSOs.

ORGANIZATIONAL AND CONTRACTUAL

I. *LEGAL ENTITY—§1851(a)(2)*

A. Provide information regarding how the applicant is organized under state law. Include a description of the entity's mission, i.e., a mission statement. If the applicant does business as (d.b.a.) a name or names different from the name shown on its Articles of Incorporation, provide such name(s) and include a copy of state approval for the d.b.a.(s) in the Documents part. Provide the name the plan will use to market its Medicare product.

B. Include in the Documents part a copy of any articles of incorporation, bylaws and other legal entity documentation. If applicable, provide the Partnership Agreement in the Documents part.

II. *STATE AUTHORITY—§1855(a)(1) and (2)*

List names, addresses, and telephone numbers of appropriate state regulatory officials who have authority to regulate health plans in the state(s) where the applicant operates. Include the names and telephone numbers of key staff.

III. *ORGANIZATION CHARTS*

Provide the following organizational charts at the end of this chapter:

A. The PSO. [If a chart was the response to §I.A.l. in the PSO Structure chapter, reference the page number of the chart.]

B. The organizational relationships of the PSO, such as where there are lines of business, parent or subsidiary entities. The current contractual relationships between the PSO entity and any administrative, management, and marketing service entities.

IV. *FULL FINANCIAL RISK—§1855(b)*

Applicants must assume full financial risk for the provision of: (1) all items and services (other than hospice care) covered under Parts A and B of Medicare to persons residing in the area served by the plan; and (2) any required additional benefits with certain exceptions (below). Describe risk sharing with providers or any other parties to prospectively assume risk:

A. Describe insurance or other arrangements for the following. Provide a copy of insurance policies in the Documents part and reference the applicable pages.

B. Describe arrangements with physicians or other health care professionals, health care institutions, or any combination of such individuals or institutions to assume all or part of the financial risk on a prospective basis for the provision of basic health services by the physicians or other health professionals or through the institutions.

C. Disclose any physician incentive plans (PIP) that the applicant has in place with contracted providers and suppliers. See guidance and forms for PIP disclosure on HCFA's web site: *http://www.hcfa.gov/medicare/mgdcar1.htm* Please complete these disclosure forms and include these completed forms in the Documents part. (§1853(j)(4)) [This form is a separate file *98dscfrm.pip*; place a hard copy in the Documents part.]

D. Legal-1 Table is a summary of insurance or other arrangements for major types of loss and liability. Fill in the table to indicate the types of arrangements in effect or to be in effect for the proposed area when qualified. [This table is a separate file *legal-1.tbl*; place a hard copy in the Documents part.]

V. *CONTRACTS FOR MANAGEMENT SERVICES*

List and briefly describe each contract for management services. Include a copy of each management contract in the Documents part of the application. Specify whether any are specific to Medicare.

VI. *PROVIDER CONTRACTS AND AGREEMENTS*

Note: For purposes of simplicity and completing this application, the term "provider" is inclusive of physicians, inpatient institutions and other ancillary practitioners. This definition departs from traditional Medicare definitions of "providers" (hospitals and other inpatient institutions, plus home health services) and "suppliers" (physicians or other practitioners and other non-providers).

There must be documentation of arrangements for health services in the requested service area at the time the application is submitted. Arrangements with providers are to be in writing. A written agreement is evidence that a health delivery network is operational and able to provide health services to enrollees. These arrangements are typically provider contracts, but may also include letters of agreement. Evidence may be the explicit inclusion of service to Medicare members and/or specific payment arrangements for services to Medicare members in provider contracts.

Complete Legal-2 table, "Provider Arrangements," for each proposed area to show the provider agreements. [This table is a separate file *legal2.xls*; place a hard copy in the Documents part. Instructions for this table are at the end of this chapter.]

In the Documents part, provide one copy of each category of provider contract between the applicant and its primary contractors, i.e., group, IPA, PHO, hospitals, skilled nursing facilities, etc. **Contracts must be executed at the time the application is submitted.**

For provider contracts and agreements between groups, IPAs, PHOs, etc., and individual subcontracting providers, provide one copy of each applicable subcontract in the Documents part. (Example: An applicant contracts with and IPA and the IPA in turn contracts with individual providers. In this instance, provide one copy of the applicable subcontract with the individual providers.) Applicants must demonstrate that all contractual provisions carry through to the level of provider actually rendering service to Medicare beneficiaries.

Note: Do not include the executed signature pages when there are multiple providers who have signed contracts that are substantially the same.

VII. *LEGAL ACTIONS*

Give a brief explanation and status of each legal action against the health care provider or group of affiliated providers that organize and operate the PSO applicant.

ON SITE DOCUMENTATION

Have the following documentation available for inspection at the site visit:

1. Articles of Incorporation, and other legal entity documentation
2. Evidence of marketing licenses or approvals
3. Executed physician, hospital, and other provider contracts fully amended for Medicare
4. Board and committee meeting minutes

5. Policy and procedures manuals

INSTRUCTIONS FOR LEGAL TABLE

LEGAL-2 PROVIDER ARRANGEMENTS

Instructions:

Provide a separate table for each county or partial county.

Column Explanations:

1. **Category—Staff/Group/IPA/PHO/Direct**:

   Member Physicians—Licensed Medical Doctors (M.D.) and Doctors of Osteopathic Medicine (O.D.) who are members of the entity.

   Member Non-Physicians—Mid-wives, nurse practitioners, or chiropractors, etc. who are members of the entity.

   Non-Member Physicians—Licensed M.D. and D.O. who are subcontracted to provide services to the entity.

   Non-Member, Non-Physician—Mid-wives, nurse practitioners, or chiropractors, etc., who are subcontracted to provide services to the entity but are not members of the entity.

   Direct Contract HMO-Physicians—Licensed M.D. and D.O. who have entered into a contract with the HMO.

2. **Type of Agreement**—Only contracts or Letters of Agreement (LOA) are acceptable. *Letters of intent are not acceptable.*
3. **Number of Agreements**—List the total number of signed agreements.
4. **Automatic Renewal of Agreements**—Provide "Yes" or "No" response.

5. **Date Executed**—Enter the date all agreements were finalized for the particular category.

6. **Page Number in Contract**—List the page number where the agreement is located in the application package.

HEALTH SERVICES DELIVERY

I. *HEALTH CARE PROVIDERS—Physician Services, Hospital Admitting Privileges—§1852(d)(1)*

   A. Describe how health care services will be provided for Medicare members, i.e., through staff, medical group, and/or IPA, direct contract, or combination.

   B. Complete PSOHSD-1& 1A Tables, *Service Area Summary of Physicians by Specialty in the Aggregate and Summary of Physicians by Specialty by County.* [Complete these tables on separate files *psohsd1.xls, psohsd1a.xls;* place a hard copy in the Documents part. Instructions for tables are at the end of this chapter.]

II. *LOCATIONS OF HEALTH SERVICES PROVIDERS—§1852(d)(1)*

   A. Complete PSOHSD-2 Table, *Provider List, by County.* Submit Microsoft Excel spread sheet format (diskette) only, not in hard copy. [Complete this table in its file *psohsd2.xls* on the disk.]

   B. Complete PSOHSD-3 Table, *Hospitals and Other Contracting Providers.* [Complete this table in its file *psohsd3.xls;* place a hard copy in the Documents part.]

III. *MEDICARE HEALTH BENEFITS—§1852(a)(1)*

   A. Complete PSOHSD-4 Table, *Direct Arrangements for Medicare Required Services.* [Complete this table in its file *psohsd4.xls;* place a hard copy in the Documents part.]

B. Complete PSOHSD-5 Table, *Arrangements for Additional and Supplemental ACR Benefits—For Medicare.* [Complete this table in its file *psohsd5.xls*; place the hard copy in the Documents part.]

C. *Medicare Materials—§1851(h)(2) and §1851(h)(3)* Provide copies of the following in the Documents part:
   - Subscriber agreement/Evidence of coverage
   - Member handbook
   - Application form
   - Disenrollment form
   - Membership card
   - Brochures/Advertising materials
   - Radio/TV scripts
   - Enrollment and disenrollment letters
   - Provider lists
   - Claims payment/denial notices
   - Correspondence relating to grievances/appeals
   - Authorization/referral forms
   - Materials prepared by affiliates and non-affiliates.

   Note: Draft copies or mark-ups should be submitted because HCFA review and approval are required before use.

D. *Compliance with State Consumer Protection and Quality Standards (§422.378)* Federally waived PSOs must comply with all state consumer protection and quality standards that would apply if it were licensed under state law, are generally applicable to other M+C organizations and plans and are consistent with M+C requirements. Such standards do not include benefit requirements, requirements relating to inclusion or treatment of providers or coverage determinations (including related appeals and grievance process). Describe in detail all State consumer protection and quality standards with which the PSO applicant must comply.

E. *State-Mandated Member Grievance and Appeals Procedures - §1852(f); 1855(g)* Explain any state-mandated member grievance and appeals procedures and how they will be available to Medicare members. As noted above, Federally waived PSOs do not have to comply with state-mandated grievance procedures relating to coverage determinations. Therefore, only describe state-mandated grievance procedures that do not relate to coverage determinations. Furthermore, provide and/or describe PSO policies and procedures for enforcing applicable state-mandated grievance procedures. Clearly explain steps and time limits for each step for the resolution of a complaint or grievance. These procedures should be placed in the Documents part of the application.

F. *Medicare Reconsideration Appeals-Hearings—§1852(g)(1)(B); 1852(g)(2)(A); 1852(g)(3)(A) and (B)* Explain the Medicare reconsideration and appeals procedures, including expedited determinations and expedited reconsideration. Explain when these procedures will be applied in place of the member grievance procedure. Provide a copy of the applicant's procedures in the Documents part.

G. *Coverage of Out-Of-Network Services—Emergency and Urgently-Needed Services; renal dialysis services; and maintenance care or post stabilization care—§1852(d)(1) and (2)* Describe your procedures for honoring, processing and paying claims for services provided to Medicare members for out-of-plan emergency and out-of-area urgently needed care, renal dialysis services, and maintenance care / post stabilization care services. Specify how coverage will be provided for emergency services, without regard to prior authorization or whether the provider is a participating provider.

H. *Coverage of Out-Of-Network Services—Point-Of-Service Benefit—§1852(d)(1)* Will Medicare members be permitted to go outside the plan for services other than emergency, renal dialysis, maintenance/post stabilization care, and authorized referrals?

If appropriate, indicate if the applicant intends to offer a Point-Of-Service (POS) benefit to Medicare members. Applicants that intend to offer a POS benefit must meet all applicable requirements for offering a POS benefit described in the Operational Policy Letter OPL96.037. *(NOTE: All OPLs are available at HCFA's web site—see Introduction)*

I. *Patient Self-Determination Amendments—§1852(I)* Explain the plan's process of providing information regarding advance directives at the time of a member's enrollment. Provide forms in the Documents part.

J. *Working Aged Enrollees* Describe the systems, policies and procedures for identifying and reporting its working aged enrollees.

IV. *UTILIZATION CONTROL PRACTICES—§1852(e)(2)*

A. Describe procedures for monitoring utilization, control costs and achieve utilization goals for the following. (NOTE: We anticipate that all Medicare+Choice plans will be required to meet applicable service authorization and utilization review standards articulated in the Quality Improvement System for Managed Care (QISMC) document.)

1. In-plan and out-of-plan physician services
2. Laboratory services
3. X-ray services
4. Hospital services, including admitting practices and length of stay
5. Out-of-area hospital services

The applicant's utilization review protocol should be (1) based on current standards of medical practice and (2) should incorporate mechanisms to detect both under and over-utilization of services. Provide the applicant's protocols for utilization review in the Documents part.

B. Detail current experience, if applicable, and projected assumptions for hospital utilization and ambulatory visits for both Medicare and non-Medicare enrollees (if applicable). Give the current community hospitalization inpatient bed-day utilization statistics for Medicare and for non-Medicare populations. (Provide name of source and the date of information).

V. *AVAILABILITY, ACCESSIBILITY AND CONTINUITY OF SERVICES—§1852(d)*

In general, plans may select the providers through whom benefits are provided. Certain stipulations must nonetheless be met (below):

A. How does the applicant assure that all covered services, including additional or supplemental services contracted by or on behalf of Medicare, are available and accessible.

B. Indicate how, when medically necessary, the plan makes benefits available and accessible 24 hours a day, 7 days a week.

C. The organization must maintain a network of providers, supported by written arrangements, that is sufficient to provide timely access to covered services. Demonstrate how the plan provides access to appropriate providers, including credentialed specialists, for medically necessary care.

D. What are the hours of operation at locations where health care services are provided?

E. How does the plan assure continuity of care for all health care services it provides to members?

F. Describe procedures for handling members who leave the service area longer than what is permitted under plan membership rules.

G. Describe the health plan's record keeping system through which pertinent information relating to health care of enrollees is accumulated and is readily available to appropriate professionals.

VI. *QUALITY ASSURANCE—§1852(e)*

A. Medicare+Choice organizations must have arrangements for an ongoing quality assurance program for health care services. Describe the applicant's quality assurance program, and specify how this program meets the following requirements:

1. Stresses health outcomes and provides for the collection, analysis and reporting of data that will permit measurement of outcomes and other quality indices;
2. Provides review by physicians and other health care professionals of the processes followed in the provision of such health care services;
3. Monitors and evaluates high volume and high risk services and the care of acute and chronic conditions;
4. Evaluates the continuity and coordination of care that enrollees receive;
5. Is evaluated on an ongoing basis as to its effectiveness;
6. Includes measures of consumer satisfaction;
7. Provides the Secretary with such access to information collected as may be appropriate to monitor and ensure the quality of care provided;
8. Provides for the establishment of written protocols for utilization review, based on current standards of medical practice;

9. Has mechanisms to detect both underutilization and over utilization of services;
10. After identifying areas for improvement, establishes or alters practice parameters;
11. Takes action to improve quality and assesses the effectiveness of such action through systematic follow-up; and
12. Makes available information on quality and outcomes measures to facilitate beneficiary comparison and choice of health coverage options.

Further, describe the following as they relate to the plans' quality assurance program:

1. The goals of the program and the organizational arrangements to carry out the program.
2. For the first year of operations under a Medicare contract, the specific objectives for the Medicare program portion and timetable for implementation.

B. Medicare+Choice applicants who demonstrate accreditation in the areas of internal quality assurance, confidentiality and accuracy of enrollee records by a private organization, which has been approved by HCFA, may be deemed to meet these requirements. If the applicant has such accreditation, check all that apply:

Plan received accreditation for internal quality assurance: yes___ no___

Plan received accreditation for confidentiality: yes___ no___

Plan received accreditation for accuracy of enrollee records: yes___ no___

Name of accrediting organization: ____________________

Provide documentation of accreditation in the Documents part of the application. §1852(e)(4))

C. Medicare+Choice plans must maintain a written agreement with a utilization and quality control peer review organization (PRO), which has a contract with the Secretary or with an entity selected by the Secretary. Specify any action that the applicant has taken to enter into such an agreement with a PRO, and/ or indicate the applicant's intentions to secure such an agreement by the time the applicant would sign any contract(s) with the Secretary as a Medicare+Choice entity.

ON-SITE DOCUMENTATION

Have the following available for inspection at the site visit:

1. Authorization/Referral forms for enrolled populations and Medicare, if different.
2. Encounter forms
3. Policy manuals
4. The organization's quality assurance program and implementation plan
5. Minutes of utilization review and quality assurance committees
6. Evidence that institutional providers are certified under Titles XVIII or XIX of the Social Security Act

INSTRUCTIONS FOR THE HEALTH SERVICES DELIVERY TABLES

PSOHSD-1 SERVICE AREA SUMMARY OF PHYSICIANS BY SPECIALTY TABLE, FOR THE ENTIRE SERVICE AREA:

Instructions:

Providers should only be counted once on this table.

Other practitioners are defined as a nurse practitioner, physician assistant or nurse mid-wife.

Column Explanations:

1. **Specialty**—Self-explanatory.
2. **Medicare PSO Affiliated Physicians**—For each affiliated provider on the "List of Affiliated Health Care Providers" table list the number of providers by specialty. The letters at the heading of each column (A-H) should correspond with those on the "List of Affiliated Health Care Providers table." In the columns labeled "T," provide the total number of each provider specialty per affiliate. In the columns labeled "A," provide only the number of each provider specialty accepting new patients for each affiliate. If you need more affiliated physician columns, use additional copies of this table and replace the letters on the columns.
3. **Sub-Total**—Calculate "T" the total number of affiliated physicians for each specialty and "A," the total number of affiliated physicians accepting new patients for each specialty.
4. **Total Number Non-Affiliated Physicians**—Provide "T," the total number of non-affiliated physicians for each specialty and "A," the total number of non-affiliated physicians accepting new patients for each specialty.

5. **Total Number Medicare PSO Physicians**—Calculate "T," the total number of Medicare PSO Physicians by specialty and "A," the total number of Medicare PSO Physicians accepting new patients by specialty.

PSOHSD-1a SUMMARY OF PHYSICIANS BY SPECIALTY TABLE, BY COUNTY:

Instructions:

Provide a separate table for each county or partial county. Providers should only be counted once per county on this table even if the provider has more than one location in that county.

A mid-level practitioner is defined as a nurse practitioner, physician assistant or nurse mid-wife.

Column Explanations: Same as 1-5 above.

PSOHSD -2 PROVIDER LIST—List of Physicians and Other Practitioners, by county:

Instructions:

Provide a separate table for each county or partial county.

Array providers alphabetically by affiliated provider letter and location.

Provide *only* on a spreadsheet format on diskette; *do not* include hard copy in the application.

Column Explanations:

1. **Name of Physician or Other Practitioner** (physician assistants, nurse practitioners and nurse mid-wives).
2. **Specialty**—Self-explanatory.

3. **Affiliated Provider Letter**—Insert the letter from the "List of Affiliated Health Care Providers" table for the affiliated provider with which this individual physician is associated. Insert NAF for non-affiliated physicians or other practitioners.

4., 5. **Service Location**—Specific city, zip code, where the provider serves patients. Providers should be listed alphabetically first by "affiliated provider letter." If a provider sees patients at more than one location list each location separately. However, the provider should only be counted once on HSD Table 1.

6. **Contracted Hospital(s) Where Privileged**—Identify hospital(s) in the geographic area where the provider has admitting privileges, other than courtesy privileges. If the hospital is a PSO affiliate, provide the hospital's "affiliated provider letter" in parenthesis.

7. **Accepts New Patients?**—Provide "Yes" or "No" response

8. **Payment Arrangements—FS= Fee Schedule DFS = Discounted Fee Schedule CAP= Capitation etc.**—Identify the method used to reimburse each contracted provider.

HSD—3 HOSPITALS AND OTHER CONTRACTING PROVIDERS Skilled Nursing Facilities, Psychiatric Hospitals, Home Health, Surgical Centers, Labs, etc.

Instructions:

Provide a separate table for each county or partial county.

For radiologists/anesthesiologists/pathologists: list only those that are employees or subcontracted by the hospital/clinic, or employed by a medical group or groups.

If the hospital provides multiple services (skilled nursing facility services, home health services or end-stage renal disease services) list each service in a separate column.

Row Explanations:

1. **Name of Provider**—Enter name and type of contracted entity. List first all Hospitals then SNFs, Psychiatric Hospitals, Home Health Agencies, Surgical Centers, Labs, Rehab Facilities, and Rural Health Clinics etc.

SNF = Skilled Nursing	PH=Psychiatric Hospital
HH= Home Health	RF= Rehab Facility
RHC= Rural Health Clinic	ESRD
SC= Surgical Center	L=Lab

2. **Affiliated Provider Letter**—Insert the affiliated provider letter given to this institutional provider on the "List of Affiliated Health Care Providers" table or "NAF" if non-affiliated.
3. **Location**—Enter city/state/zip code.
4. **Payment Arrangement**—FS=Fee Schedule, DFS= Discounted Fee Schedule, CAP=Capitation etc.—Identify the method used to reimburse contracted providers
5. **Title 18 Certification # or Provider #—Self-explanatory.**
6. **Occupancy Rate**—Provide the current occupancy rate for each institutional provider.
7. **Services Provided**—In Outpatient categories enter "Yes" for all services provided. (Leave blank if not applicable.) In Inpatient categories enter actual bed count for each breakdown listed; if none, enter zero (0). (If Surgery or Coronary Care Unit bed counts are listed in previous entries, so state in box, i.e., (include above).

PSOHSD—4 DIRECT ARRANGEMENTS FOR MEDICARE REQUIRED SERVICES

Instructions:

Provide a separate table for each county or partial county.

Column Explanations:

1. **Required Services**—Self-explanatory
2. **Name & Location of Providers for Medicare Beneficiaries**—Enter provider name and address where services are provided. If provider is Group, IPA, PHO, Direct w/Plan or Staff indicate name of entity; if provided by more than one source, state all sources. Insert the affiliated provider letter from the "List of Affiliated Health Care Providers" table or NAF for non-affiliated providers.

PSOHSD—5 ARRANGEMENTS FOR ADDITIONAL AND SUPPLEMENTAL ACR BENEFITS

Instructions:

Provide a separate table for each county or partial county. Check the benefit type that is being offered.

Definitions:

Refer to the HMO/CMP Manual, Chapter 5200 and OPL95.030 for information: *Additional Benefit, Mandatory Supplemental Benefit,* or *Optional Supplemental Benefit.*

Column Explanations:

1. **Non-required ACR Benefits**—see definition section above

2. **Additional Benefit**—see definition section above
3. **Mandatory Supplemental Benefit**—see definition section above
4. **Optional Supplemental Benefit**—see definition section above
5. **Name & Location of Providers for Medicare Beneficiaries**—Enter provider name and address where services are provided. If provider is Group, IPA, PHO, Direct w/Plan or Staff indicate name of entity; if provided by more than one source, state all sources. If the service is provided by a subcontractor indicate the name of the entity.
6. **Affiliate Provider Letter**—Insert the affiliated provider letter from the "List of Affiliated Health Care Providers" table or NAF for non-affiliated providers.

FINANCIAL[1]

I. *MINIMUM NET WORTH AMOUNT—§422.382*

A. Complete and insert into the Documents part, in the format of *psofin2.xls*, the federal regulatory adjusted net worth analysis. List the PSO's Federally Adjusted Net Worth and cash and cash equivalents below.

B. Provide independently certified audited financial statements for the most recent fiscal year period in the Documents part. If the proposed M+C plan is a line of business of the PSO applicant, provide audited statements relating to the legal entity of which the PSO is a part. Audits are to include:

1. Opinion of a certified public accountant

[1]State licensed PSOs using this application must substitute the Financial chapter of the Medicare+Choice HMO, PPO application form.

2. Statement of revenues and expenses
3. Balance sheet
4. Statement of cash flows
5. Explanatory notes
6. Management letters

C. Provide in the Documents part a copy of the most recent unaudited financial statements of the entity.

D. If you included "Other Assets" (*PSOFIN2*—Federal Regulatory Net Worth Analysis, line 1.5) in the calculation of the PSO's Federally Adjusted Net Worth, briefly explain the Statutory Accounting Practices you followed. Document the Statutory Accounting Practices for HMOs used by the state in which the PSO is domiciled.

E. If applicable, describe any administrative arrangements that the entity has or has available to it which HCFA may consider appropriate to reduce, control or eliminate costs. Such arrangement might include use of parent or affiliate administrative services at little or no cost to the PSO or contracts for administrative services which are payed on a per capita basis. These arrangements must be evidenced in the entity's financial plan and documented in the Documents part.

F. Describe any subordinated debts or subordinated liabilities listed on PSOFIN2-Federal Regulatory Net Worth Analysis. Provide documentation of subordinated debts and liabilities in the Documents part.

G. If the entity is a public corporation or subsidiary of a public corporation, provide the most recent Annual Report pursuant to Section 13 or 15(d) of the Securities Exchange Act of 1934, Form 10-K in the Documents part.

H. If the entity has raised capital through public offerings within the last 3 years or anticipates a public offering, provide a copy of the prospectus in the Documents part.

II. *FINANCIAL PLAN REQUIREMENT—§422.384*

All PSO applicants must provide a financial plan that demonstrates how the legal entity will maintain fiscal soundness and continue to meet minimum net worth, liquidity and deposit requirements. The financial plan should be in the Documents part and include the following:

A. *Financial Projections* The PSO must provide projections from the anticipated effective date of the M+C contract through one year or one year beyond break-even (whichever is longer). Provide actual data (not necessarily audited statements) for the period between the date of the latest annual audit and the anticipated effective date of the M+C contract.

Financial projections should be prepared using the accrual method of accounting in conformity with generally accepted accounting principles. Include certification of reserves and actuarial liabilities by a qualified health maintenance organization actuary if this has been done. Prepare projections using the pro-forma financial statement methodology from *psofin3.xls*. Projections are to be part of the Financial Documents part and must include the following:

1. BALANCE SHEET

Format: PSOFIN3BS BALANCE SHEET (similar to NAIC Health Plan Report: Assets, Liabilities, Capital and Surplus blanks)

Frequency of Projection: The Balance Sheet should reflect data as of:

—Date of application (actual data)

—Quarterly (projected data) until one year past breakeven

—Annually (projected data) until one year past breakeven

If PSO is currently at breakeven, as indicated by an audited financial statement, then only one year of projections is required.

2. STATEMENTS OF REVENUES AND EXPENSES

Format: PSOFIN3RE REVENUE AND EXPENSE STATEMENT (similar to NAIC Health Plan Report: Statement of Revenue and Expenses, Capital and Surplus Account)

Frequency of Projections: The Statement of Revenue and Expense should reflect data as of:

—Date of application (actual data)

—Monthly (projected data) for each of the first 12 months of operation.

—Quarterly (projected data based on standard quarters) for each quarter until one year past breakeven

—Annually (projected data) until one year past breakeven

Uncovered Expenses. For all expenses indicate those expense which are uncovered and total expenses. Uncovered expenses are those expenses that are the obligation of the reporting entity, for which an enrollee may also be liable in the event of the organizations insolvency and for which no alternative arrangements have been made that are acceptable to HCFA. Such expenses may include out-of-area, referral services, and hospital services.

Segregation of expenses into covered expenses and total expenses is required only for annual projections (not monthly and quarterly projections).

Breakeven. If PSO is currently at breakeven, as indicated by an audited financial statement, then only One Year of Projections is required.

Line of business. In cases where the PSO plan is a line of business, the applicant should also complete a statement of revenue and expenses for the line-of-business.

3. STATEMENTS OF CASH FLOWS

Format: PSOFIN3CF STATEMENT OF CASH FLOWS (Indirect Method) (similar to NAIC Health Plan Report: Statement of Cash Flows [Indirect -Method])

Frequency of Projection: The Statement of Cash Flows should reflect data as of:

—Date of application (actual data)

—Quarterly (projected data) until one year past Breakeven

—Annually (projected data) until one year past Breakeven

If PSO is currently at breakeven, as indicated by an audited financial statement, then projection of only one year is required.

B. *Statement and Justification of Assumptions* State and include in the Documents part major assumptions separately for Medicare and any other pre-paid health care lines of business in sufficient detail to allow an independent financial analyst to reconstruct projected figures using only the stated assumptions. Include operating and capital budget breakdowns.

Stated assumptions should address all periods for which projections are made and include inflation assumptions. Details of minor assumptions will be verified on site. Justify assumptions to the extent that a knowledgeable reviewer would be convinced that they are reasonable. Base justification on such factors as the applicant's experience, the experience of other health plans. Describe hospital and health professional costs and utilization in detail.

For a line of business, assumptions need only be submitted to support the projections of the Medicare line and any other pre-paid health care lines.

Note: If an organization has a category of revenue and/or expense that is not included in the present definitions, provide an explanation.

C. *Statements of the availability of financial resources to meet projected losses.* Describe financing arrangements and include all documents supporting these arrangements for any projected deficits in the Documents part. Note: There must be evidence of financing arrangements for the entire projected deficit and except for letters of credit, guarantees, lines of credit and any other accepted legally binding agreements, the organization must have the resources for meeting projected losses on its balance sheet in cash or a form that is convertible to cash in a timely manner in accordance with the financial plan.

If the PSO is using guarantees, letters of credit, lines of credit or any other legally binding agreements as financing arrangements, please identify and describe these arrangements below and summarize how and when they will be used. Provide in the Documents part a signed copy of any such arrangements and the most recent independently audited financial statements for all guarantors. These financial statements must include balance sheets, profit and loss statements and cash flow statements. Note: If the PSO is using guarantees to fund projected losses it must meet the requirements of §422.390 and obtain cash or cash equivalents from the guarantor in a timely manner (see §422.384 (e) (2)). For example, the PSO must obtain from the guarantor cash or cash equivalents sufficient to fund the first two quarters of projected losses prior to the effective date of the contract

D. *Liquidity (§422.386)* A PSO must have sufficient cash flow to meet its financial obligations as they become due and payable. For the last six months of operation discuss how the organization monitors its ability to meet current obligations. Include in this discussion the balance sheet current ratio for the last six months as well as the average days to pay a claim. Describe the availability of outside financial resources to meet any liquidity shortfall.

III. *DEPOSITS (Provisions for the Event of Insolvency)—§422.388*

A. *Insolvency Deposit (§422.388 (a))* Identify below the institution with which the PSO is maintaining the $100,000 deposit in cash or securities and describe how it is restricted for use in the event of the PSO's insolvency to help assure continuation of services or pay costs associated with receivership or liquidation. Document this deposit in the Documents part.

B. *Uncovered Expenditures Deposit (§422.388 (b))*

1. Describe below provisions to protect Medicare members in the event of insolvency.

   a. To continue services for the duration of the contract period for which payment has been made and until the time of discharge for Medicare members confined in an inpatient facility.

   b. To protect Medicare members from incurring liability for services provided before the plan's insolvency.

2. In the format of *psofin1.xls* "Uncovered Expenditures Calculation Worksheet," calculate the entity's uncovered health care expenditures and uncovered expenditures as a percentage of total expenditures (see 4

below). Insert this work sheet in the Documents part. Uncovered expenditures means those expenditures for health care services that are the obligation of an organization, for which an enrollee may also be liable in the event of the organization's insolvency.

3. Provide all documents supporting arrangements to protect members in the event of the PSO's insolvency and cover uncovered expenditures in the Documents part. These arrangements include provider contract provisions not to bill members and/or continue services without payment (note the application page of these provisions), insolvency riders to reinsurance policies, letters of credit or guarantees. If applicable, include independently certified audited statements of any guarantor.

4. If more than 10% of the organization's health care expenditures are "uncovered" the organization must maintain a restricted deposit equal to 120% of the PSO's outstanding liability for uncovered expenditures. If required, please list below the amount of the uncovered expenditures deposit, the institution with which the PSO is maintaining the deposit and how it is restricted for use in the event of the PSO's insolvency. Document this deposit in the documents part.

IV. *MEDICARE SECONDARY PAYOR—§1852(a)(4)*

Describe the systems/procedures the organization will implement (1) under the Medicare Secondary Payor provisions and (2) to avoid duplicate payment of health care services.

V. *ACCOUNTING FOR INCURRED BUT NOT REPORTED CLAIMS (IBNR)*

Describe the method of accounting for claims incurred, but for which bills have not been received at the end of accounting periods.

VI. *ADJUSTED COMMUNITY RATE PROPOSAL (ACRP)*—

Submit a hard copy of the ACRP in the Document part. See the HCFA Internet site for ACR information and formats to download onto diskette.

ON SITE DOCUMENTS

Have the following available for inspection at the site visit:

1. The most recent (unaudited) financial statements to update those submitted with the application, using the same format.
2. Actuarial analysis prepared by independent actuaries if used in developing the financial assumptions.
3. Evidence of subordination of any subordinated liabilities.

MARKETING

I. *ENROLLMENT HISTORY*

By product line, describe your enrollment history since the start of operations.

II. *ENROLLMENT PROJECTIONS*

Provide quarterly enrollment projections by product line extending one year beyond the anticipated Medicare contract effective date, using the enrollment table (psoenroll.tbl) on the diskette. [Complete this table in its file *psoenroll.tbl;* place a hard copy in the Documents part.]

III. *COMPETITION*

Specify Medicare competitors' current benefits, premium levels, and market share. Provide the name and address of each competitor specified.

IV. *MARKETING STRATEGY—§1851(h)*

Describe the applicant's Medicare marketing strategy, including:

1. Overall approach in the marketplace
2. Sales approach
3. Plans for community education and public relations
4. Advertising/promotion programs
5. Systems for managing inquiries and servicing members
6. Marketing staffing
7. Marketing budget

V. *TITLES XIII AND XIX ENROLLMENT—§1851(g)*

Describe plans for conducting enrollment of Medicare beneficiaries. State the date the entity expects to begin serving Medicare members. Specify if the entity enrolls Medicaid recipients.

DOCUMENTS

THE FOLLOWING DOCUMENTS ARE FILES THAT BELONG IN THIS PART

Please be sure to:

- INCLUDE THE COMPLETED FILES ON THE DISKETTE SUBMITTED TO HCFA.
- MANUALLY INSERT COMPLETED DOCUMENTS, AS DIRECTED WITHIN THE NARRATIVE, WHEN PREPARING THE HARD COPY OF APPLICATION.
- NUMBER EACH PAGE (OR DOCUMENT) IN THE DOCUMENTATION PART.

Chapter	*File Name*	*Description*
General Information	psosetup.wpd	Medicare Set-up Forms
PSO Structure & Defining Requirements	psoprov.wpd	List of Affiliated Providers Table
	psosubst.xls	Substantial Proportion Worksheet
Organizational & Contractual	psopip98.wpd	Physician Incentive Plan Disclosure
	psoleg1.wpd	Insurance Coverage
	psoleg2.xls	Provider Arrangements
Health Services Delivery	psohsd1.xls	Summary of Physicians, Aggregate
	psohsd1a.xls	Summary of Physicians, County
	psohsd2.xls	Provider List, by County—on diskette, not hard copy
	psohsd3.xls	Hospitals, etc.
	psohsd4.xls	Medicare Required Services
	psohsd5.xls	Additional/Supplemental
Financial	psofins.xls (sheets 1–3)	Uncovered Expenditure Calculation Work Sheet, Federal Regulatory Adjusted Net Work Analysis, Financial Plan Format
Marketing	psoenrol.wpd	Enrollment Projections

INDEX

J

L

M

Q

R

U

V

W

9 780834 211773

Printed in Dunstable, United Kingdom

88190716R00159